best
monologues
from
the best
american
short
plays
volume one

best monologues from the best american short plays

volume one

edited by william w. demastes

APPLAUSE THEATRE & CINEMA BOOKS
An Imprint of Hal Leonard Corporation

Published in 2014 by Applause Theatre & Cinema Books
An Imprint of Hal Leonard Corporation
7777 West Bluemound Road
Milwaukee, WI 53213

Trade Book Division Editorial Offices
33 Plymouth St., Montclair, NJ 07042

Printed in the United States of America

Book design by Lynn Bergesen

Library of Congress Cataloging-in-Publication Data

Best Monologues from The Best American Short Plays, Volume One /
edited by William W. Demastes.
        pages cm. -- (The Applause Acting Series)
    1. Monologues, American. 2. American drama--20th century. 3. American
drama--21st century. I. Demastes, William W., editor of compilation.
    PS627.M63B47 2014
    812'.04508--dc23
                                2013041949

ISBN 978-1-4803-3155-6

www.applausebooks.com

contents

introduction

Thespis Steps Out

Somewhere in the deepest recesses of prehistory, a lone intrepid human being stepped out of the safe confines of some huddled mass and announced himself to the world as an individual, someone who could stand alone and was capable of thinking, fighting, loving, fending for himself. Whoever that first person was, he took a singular action that has defined human beings ever since, a species that best survives as a group but remains determined to take on the world by rejecting the anonymous comfort and safety of the herd, or tribe, or community. The anonymity of a group may be synonymous with safety, but humans seem bent on defying the benefits of running with the pack, choosing instead the death-defying option of stepping out of the ranks and testing the limits of individual human endurance, courage, and foolhardiness.

Truth be told, most of us do work to squeeze into the comforting center of our tribe, engaging in that choral huddle that seems to guarantee longevity at the expense of distinction. After all, life and the arts that imitate it remind us time and again that the price of distinction is often too high, that the cost of independence is sometimes life itself. But even then, we often still go against our better instincts and celebrate the standout, honoring his triumphs and mourning his losses. Even against our common sense we celebrate the bold, brazen foolhardiness of the risk taker. He captures our imagination as he expands the definition of what it is to be human, showing us the godlike glory of our reach even as he reveals the earthbound limits of our grasp.

More than any other art form, theater captures this elemental human quality, celebrating the individual who steps out of the chorus, defines himself by shaking his spear at the world, and rejects the panicked instinct to retreat from what lies before him. Greek mythology calls that first bold individual Thespis, the first human to step out of the crowd and face yet another crowd—an audience—as he shared the truth about human nature with his fellows. That's what actors have done ever since. Much has transpired on the stage since then, but it is always the actor who faces an audience that stands at the heart of the matter. And that is exactly why monologues are so important not just to art or the theater, but to the continued rejuvenation and regeneration of human nature itself. Standing forth, pulling together a spotlighted performance that capitalizes on the honest vulnerabilities of the actor while standing before a mass of onlookers—that comes as close to the full and complex spirit of Thespis as currently exists in the human world today.

The spirit of the brave individual facing a scrutinizing crowd without the life support of a chorus or supporting cast is what the contents of this book celebrates. The monologue tests the limits of human individuality, exposing a wide variety of human qualities by moving very private conversations into the public sphere. Sharing these certain private conversations with intimate friends—or holding those thoughts altogether for exclusively personal consideration—is the stoic and generally accepted way of doing things. Breaking through that façade, however, is what the monologist does. He or she shares truths that make us all a bit uncomfortable because of the very public nature of this otherwise private transaction. But when it works, the event runs full circle by moving from publicly exposed individual vulnerabilities to a point where community itself is reinstituted. The monologue may begin with the individual, but it ends with a webwork of relationships between the monologist and audience that seems the very antithesis of the original enterprise. On the face of it, it seems counterintuitive to think that this confessional mode would do anything other than expose the individual to scarlet condemnation and deserved ostracism. But when done well, monologues take individual exposure and unite humans in bonds of shared experiences—shared celebrations, shared commiserations, shared fears, and shared ambitions either accomplished or abandoned. Whether or not this was the intention behind Thespis's bold step forward, it certainly has been the result.

• • • •

This is a collection of monologues drawn from the popular The Best American Short Plays series, an archive of works

from many of the best playwrights active today. The monologues selected for this volume present taut, engaging single-
character pieces that range from zany comedy to poignant
tales of love and loss. Many included pieces are excerpted from
the plays of this series while others are by design full and complete monologues. Long or short, serious or not, excerpts or
otherwise, this collection includes works that capture much of
what it means to be human, particularly that urge to stand out
and sing our successes and failures, hopes and fears.

—William W. Demastes
Louisiana State University

best
monologues
from
the best
american
short
plays
volume one

Part I

Monologues for Men

Susan Miller

excerpt from

Reading List

from

The Best American
Short Plays 2004–2005

The stars. I was looking up anything I could find on the stars.
There was this article about dark matter that scared the shit
out of me, and I was putting my whole family through hell
about it. Just the way my daughter has pushed me to my
limits with her inquiries into the absurdity of language and
meaning. Meaning there is none. No meaning. Which I take
as bleak and troublesome coming like that from a young
person. And, I guess, it challenged something deep and
confronted me on a personal level. Like my fatherhood, my
being a parent was all of a sudden a pointless and sorry thing.
I like talking at the dinner table. It's time well spent if you put
aside other concerns. But I was depressing everyone, and I
thought maybe there's another way, you know, with more
information, to look at things. To look at this dark matter and
my daughter's questions and turn it all into a metaphor of

well-being instead of what it clearly represented to me now as a crushing void with the power to cancel the present, past, and future. Life, albeit the sad and confusing thing though it is, still, it is what we know. And what we want our children to know. Well, apparently in my investigations of the universe there were more than a couple of references to a certain gay astronomer. He kept turning up in the materials I happened to look through. And they wanted to know—*they* being the messengers of secrecy and harbingers of silence—what I had to do with him. What interest did I have in a gay astronomer who was fired from his post in the fifties, and what business did I have with footnotes that referred to the incident in the park, and did I know him.

Billy Aronson

excerpt from

Little Red Riding Hood

from

The Best American Short Plays 1992–1993

NOTE:

MOTHER's prompting words
can be spoken offstage.

HUNTER   If a hunter doesn't have his slab o' steak he can't grab his gun and if he can't grab his gun he can't blast the beasts and if he can't blast the beasts how's he gonna market their meats if he can't market their meats there's no way he can house his spouse and if he can't house his spouse then where's he supposed to eat his slab o' steak, in the gosh darn mud crap slop?

MOTHER   *You didn't get one of your arms into your shirt, dear.*

HUNTER   Sure you miss a sleeve now and then or
sometimes you forget to button a few buttons, but what about
the sleeve you did get into the shirt, what about the buttons
you did button. I'm sick and tired of people who always focus
on the empty sleeve or the unbuttoned button.

MOTHER   *Your fly's open.*

HUNTER   or the opened fly, when the fact is if the truth
be known when push comes to shove it's the people with the
unbuttoned buttons and unsleeved arms who are out there
not looking at the lookers who are looking at them but just
plain out there being out there. I'm out there. [...] I'm the
one who faces the heat and the snow and the dirt—and let
me tell you it gets dirty—so I can brave the hills and the
lakes and the pebbles—which inevitably get in your boots—
to grapple with the branches and the ragweed and the
pollen—'til I'm sneezin' my head off—don't make me remind
you about the time I got poison oak all across the cheeks o'
my butt—do you have any idea how filthy my toenails get by
the end of the day?—and why? So I can shoot the beasts that
make the coats that coat the backs of the very people who
stand there staring at my empty sleeve when they should
have been paying more attention to the arm in their own
backyard in the first place.

MOTHER   *There's grease on your nose and steak on your fore-head, and your fork is lodged behind your ear.*

HUNTER   What's a drop o' grease on a hunter's nose for the sake of his home, or a fork in his ear for his family? I love this fork and I love this family and let me tell you something, sister, I may have a slab of greasy beef suspended from my brow but that won't stop me from pumping ten ounces of lead into a fat-assed quadruped at close range because it's a dog eat dog jungle in that forest.

Carol K. Mack

excerpt from

The Courier

from

The Best American
Short Plays 2005–2006

YOUNG MAN   The packages. They were all sealed. And
every day there was a new one. I was taking them to a lab. All
these boxes, sealed red boxes. Shiny. Nothing could leak out
but…all going from Central to this lab, see? After a coupla
months I wonder who's it going to? And what's in the boxes?
He never said nothing about that. I think maybe it's O.K. if I
know what's inside a' them? I mean, it don't make no
difference. I'd always do my job. Do my best! Like he said. All
I did was take off the label. Not even get the tape off. Just the
label. No name. Some kind of bar-code label. I just start to
take it off with my penknife.

[*Very odd mechanical noise.* YOUNG MAN *startled, stands.*]

And before I know it these guys show up, see? Then I get
arrested for possession of lethal materials. They accuse me of

planning a terrorist attack. They say the box contains a biological weapon. I say that's not possible. They say, "Who do you work for?" I tell them I take the package from Central to the lab. I tell them that's my job. They tell me there **IS** no lab. They tell me there is no central nothing. That they don't exist and they never have. Then I figure O.K., O.K., this has gotta be some kinda test. Right? Maybe they test you every month. So then they say, "Who do you work for?" and I say, "What?" And they say, "Who do you work for?" and I say, "I...I used to work for the U.S. Post Office and I don't work for *nobody* now," and they say, "Then who told you to do it?"

[*Breaking down, in tears.*]

And I say, "Do *what*?" Do WHAT? For chrissakes' I trusted them. I *believed* in them. I was selected for this job and now they turn against me for *what*.

David Kranes

excerpt from

Going In

from

The Best American
Short Plays 1986

JONAS   I try to instruct the world—and myself, through
the reminders of that instruction—in the elegance of what
any of us might reach for! What's attainable!...My
communication tends to...I use a baroque language, because
I feel that a baroque language, possibly, is best-suited for...!
Be sure that milk's put away! I'll take responsibility for the
cheese. When you wake up in the morning, in the dawn of a
new day, I guarantee that the brie will be in its proper
place!...Don't shrug! Don't slouch! Don't break training!
And if you try to change any of the records in *this* room—I'll
be waiting for you! So plan your attack!...Or attack your
plan! And remember that any of us are our own plans! So
execute well! Because I am not alone! And Hank Williams is
armed. And Don and Phil Everly are *contenders* again. […] "I
coulda been a contender."

[*Out.*]

Who *said* that?!... Wrong! It was *not* Rocky Balboa.... Well, I do love you! If I'm forced to answer my own question, which has generally been the story of my life. I also do not—*not*—love you! So there! There! All my questions are answered! All my holes are filled! *Some* of my holes are filled!

[*To himself.*]

And some of my holes *better not* be filled... or I'm in trouble. Because I tend to do things "in excess" when the first blush is on... and then, ultimately, in moderation. But I love my son—and that will have to do for this evening, thank you. Thank you. Thank You. You're welcome, I'm sure. Good night.

Joe Maruzzo

excerpt from

Bricklayer's Poet

from

The Best American
Short Plays 2007–2008

Don't think I'm crazy or nothin', you see, I'm a very practical
kind of guy, black and white, right side of the brain and all
that, but this last fireplace I did, I'm doin' this fireplace for
the Corsos, sweet old people from Brooklyn, Sal and Bunny
Corso, I know them all my life. Sal's in *his* eighties and he's
dying of cancer, rest his soul, so Bunny calls me and she wants
him to have a fireplace before he goes, something he always
wanted. But at the time I was going through some stuff in my
life, and the last thing I wanted to do in the middle of August
was a fireplace. It was like 120 degrees in there! I'm doin' the
job for practically nothin', I charged them just for the
material, and I'm like a day into it. And I realize the wall's on
a slant, it's crooked. I had to do all this special chipping and
slanting the stone, the Corsos are sittin' right in back of me
watchin' my every move, not out of thinking I was gonna

screw them or anything, but that they were happy watchin'
their fireplace go up! So there I am, the sweat's pourin' out of
me, my mind is racin' about my life, my father, and I'm lifting
this eightypound stone towards the wall, but it won't take, it
won't stick. And I feel this pain in my heart, like a stake
runnin' through me, and I can't move, I'm as stiff as a board,
and all of a sudden my body starts to come up out of me! I
swear to God ! My body is leaving me! And its goin' up
through the ceiling, into the sky, but I can still see myself
down there, I could see the Corsos, but I'm goin' higher and
higher with all these puffy white clouds, and I hear this
humming, this humming of something holy, like kids singin'
this sweet sound, and I feel a tickle on my ear, and I turn and
there's this angel with the wings and this beautiful little baby
face, it's floatin' there and it whispers into my ear, "Love,
Mikey, don't forget love." And all of a sudden I was back on
the ground, holding the stone like I never left, but I'm cryin',
I'm cryin' like a friggin' baby, so I run to the bathroom 'cause
I don't want the Corsos to think I was cracking up, and
everything got peaceful, and I hear that voice again sayin',
"Love, Mikey, don't forget love." I walked out, went back to
my fireplace, and it was the most beautiful fireplace I ever
laid. I got a picture of it, you wanna see it? [...] That's me.
That's Sal and Bunny. That's the fireplace. It's lovely. [...]
You're the first person I told about this. That's all I gotta do is
talk to the guys in the neighborhood, they'd think I was nuts.
I usually don't talk to them about private things. That voice,

it was my father. He was tellin' me it's gonna be all right. He was tellin' me to love. [...] He was a bricklayer. Taught me everything I know. Talk about hands. He had a pair of hands so gentle, he'd hold a brick like it was a piece of cake, so smooth, you couldn't even tell he was layin' a brick, like cream. He'd take a brick, you know, he'd chip it because there'd be a problem with the fireplace, so he'd chip the brick and the whole thing would go straight up. He was a craftsman. And clean! When he got through, you think he hired a cleaning lady. They don't make 'em like that no more. He was a little guy, short and stocky, green eyes, light brown hair, and whenever you were in trouble, he was there! If you needed a buck or two, his hand was in his pocket, if a guy needed a day's work, he'd hire him for the week, even if he took the loss. Anyway, it's a funny thing we're talkin' about these things and all, but lately, I feel like I need to talk to somebody like I gotta share things, inside me, with them. Maybe it's my age or something, but I feel it's time [...] to settle down. Maybe not marriage and all but to live with at least. I'll tell ya, I look around and I see a lot of lonely people. I think if they made a study or somethin', they'd find out there are more people alone in the world than ever before. Well, at least in this city.

Julia Jarcho

excerpt from

The Highwayman

from

The Best American
Short Plays 2005–2006

HIGHWAYMAN   One wants to say something, I mean.
Here's the floor. Thanks. You want to keep people's hopes up,
when you can, that's not, I'll admit that's not the first thing on
one's mind all the time. I've tried to dress in a way that'd be
appropriate to passing by at a gallop or stopping and saying
"dismount." People don't always know what that means. This
is a strange area. I've traveled, I travel a long ways, and it's
hard to say where I'm originally from. They're entranced
from the first word and I don't like to disagree. There's so
much of the same for them. It's the same by the ocean as it is
on the moor. In my opinion, a trance is what they're after. It
seems to me to be the wrong prize. The last man I killed, I'd
gotten him in the belly and he dropped his gun. So he asked
me to. Or music. I find both of these helpful in trying to
understand. But at the same time, I've never been entranced.

It might have to do with the motion of the horse. Air blowing by. Through. And the night: at nighttime, light always changes. I mean, and the maneuvering keeps you unkept.

[*Beat.*]

It usually goes like this: they're riding and I'm riding. I pull mine out in front. I say, "Stop. Give me everything you're carrying." And I don't give exceptions. They'll try to lie, but I can tell when they've been comfortable. When people have too much it sits ill on them. They're better off without it. Sometimes that can refer to the most essential things. Sometimes it's their hair. Sometimes some of their clothes. I have an idea, which I see as a picture, and in it the world is almost empty, and everyone I see is just the bare bones of a self, staggering through bright weather between days.

Mark Medoff

excerpts from

DeBoom: Who Gives This Woman?

from

The Best American Short Plays 2006–2007

GEOFFREY DeBOOM   Used to be I slept six hours and erupted into the day, my mind as febrile at the moment of tremulous waking as it would be in the epicenter of the day's quakes. Now, I sleep and wake and sleep eight, nine, ten hours and have no desire to get out of bed except for the middle-of-the-night urination—and then only for the sake of my decaying kidneys (27 percent function last test)—the lack of desire to rise and go forth abetted, no doubt, by the fact that I have nothing to look forward to, or to be fair— not that fair is of much interest to me anymore—that I look forward to nothing. I roll off the Posturepedic so as not to

precipitate a back spasm that would put me back to bed for
a couple of weeks, forced to choose among self-analysis,
pop books, bad music, or, worse, movies. So I would rather
go to the university than stay home. Thus, mobility, such as
it is, has value. I engineer the four-step journey across carpet
into the bathroom, favoring the titanium and plastic right
knee over the left one with its shards of chipped bone and
cartilage roaming the joint like Rice Krispies through
molasses. Load my toothbrush with whitening paste and
crane myself toward the toilet with stiff arms on the seat,
dropping lead-like the last few inches as my arms give out
to gravity.

Avoid the mirror. Pee lefty, brush righty. Wait for my
indolent bladder to drain. Pee, squeeze, squirt, squeeze, sit,
wait, wait, dribble, squeeze, squirt. I stopped frequenting the
student bathroom down the hall from my garret in favor of a
trek to the faculty lav several corridors over, following a whiz
between two undergrads who imagined life would always be
thus, their bladders emptying in a tsunami of malted urine.
They left me chained to the urinal like Prometheus, long
after they'd zipped, washed (one of them), exited (lunch, ball
game, sexual encounter?), while I stood and sprinkled and
spritzed for a couple of hours, guilty of what wisdom has
taught is mankind's most egregious sin: growing old. I drive
off the toilet on a silent "Hut!," aware that no matter how
many last little squeezes I exert on my prostate, before I am
upright my penis will emit a last squirt that will saturate a

quarter size circle in the crotch of my Jockeys. (Tip: black underwear.) Limp the road of life now with wet pants. On a panel at a civil rights conference last year on the failure of the movie industry to do much about diversity (and in a superficial effort at disclosure—not there as a supporter of affirmative action, political correctness, or the glories of the melting pot; I was there to say the industry was not a moral conglomerate but a financial one that didn't care about diversity unless it paid in dollars). Wearing cream-colored Zanellas. Knew, following the pre-speech safety whiz; I'd spritz a 25-cent piece right before taking the stage. Wore a Kotex Mini Pad.

Diapers pretty soon. Rinse toothpaste—two cupped palms of water, left above right— always two, going back to age eight and the onset of compulsive behavior: Save the family, give thanks to a benevolent Savior, request not to die young. Shake out the toothbrush, restore it to its place in the receptacle next to Cass's unused, firm Oral-B. I had figured in twisted Cartesian fashion: She has a toothbrush at my condo; therefore, she'll come back to me.

Must tackle my image in the mirror (daily query delivered to no one but me: What is my father doing in there?) and resist with the modicum of self-control still available the desire to smash my head through glass, plaster board, and studs to the outdoors. Imagine my father's and my communal head, connected by a tendon or two, yo-yoing from the second floor.

Next, a moment's loathing of the once sculpted but now flaccid pecs (pubescent breasts, really), the reedy biceps, their rippling, dry overskin like stretched, faux snake skin, the leavened baguette in the midriff that defies the hundreds of crunches I do daily.

My eyes drop to the ellipse-shaped pouches under my eyes that don't go away since squirrels started depositing their nuts there a decade back. Not tiredness, according to a woman at a book signing, she with parchment skin stretched like loomed silk over the front of her skull and tacked behind her ears, but, she whispered so that only the first five or so in line behind her could hear, the walnuts are just fat deposits which can be removed in an hour operation in a doctor's office.

Tropical forests of hair festoon along the helix, tragus, lobe of my ears, sprout like roach antennae from the tip of my nose. Every two weeks, with tweezers, I stand here wearing my reading glasses and pluck the antennae black filament by black filament, each pluck sending through my neural network a little electrical reminder of my putrefaction.

There is the hair on my head that only recently began thinning on top and receding into my temples. Good chance death will beat baldness.

The human body, helpless to resist, humiliates the living thing that was itself. I have contemplated suicide a thousand, ten thousand times. I have stood on three separate Saturday afternoons at Barnes & Noble and perused the periodically updated tome that details for do-it-yourself sorts the best ways to get it done. Tell myself I can't kill myself because of Cass and Maxine.

• • • •

GEOFFREY DeBOOM   My life insurance might not pay off, as if that's an issue, since my daughter is rich and can take care of her mother, whether she wins a Nobel Prize or not, if she lives another hundred years. But I know, though once unafraid if not brave, I am a coward now and don't have the guts. A Southern Baptist gone public atheist, I am a closet Catholic. I fear there's a hell to which I'll be assigned for eternity with all the other perfidious misanthropes who set themselves up as judges of mass culture. Terror keeps me alive, witness to my deterioration.

Dressed, deodorized, pomaded, I limp to the kitchen, listing to port, the left leg three-eights of an inch shorter than the right since the right knee was replaced with plastic and titanium. At the out-of-fashion tile counter I commence the ceremony of the pills. Seven supplements shipped via UPS once a month from a distributor in Dallas, then the replacement for the pill for arthritis that was destroying my kidneys and the one for high blood pressure followed by the one for the hyperthyroidism that is trying to keep the kidney function I have at its current short-of-dialysis level.

Skip the antidepressant for the eighteenth straight day.

I turn on my computer. Download e-mail. There are nineteen. Several from students with work attached; the *New York Times*; Truthout, a website I use to keep track of liberal—pardon me, progressive—bullcrap; one from Max ("I need to talk to you, but we have to leave for the airport."), a couple of ads, three reminders of meetings at the Film School, two of which I'll duck though I've confirmed I'll attend.

Responding to e-mail has become my substitute for writing reviews, the thing I did for a living several times a week for thirty years, or writing the copy for my TV show, which I did for a decade and a half. I drag it out, to minimize guilt for not working on the column I still write monthly for *Esquire*, until I can go to school but not be there so long that I'm bored or have to talk to people I don't want to talk to—which takes in pretty much everyone there. The phone rings at seven forty-two. I have no message, just the "beep." […]

I wait to board last. Fester past the fortunate eight who fill the spacious elite seats with their smug complacence toward me, hunched like Quasimodo, nudging as if I were in ankle shackles to the back of the plane, where I'll be crammed in three abreast with insufficient room for my failing body parts.

At my row will be a colossus who runneth over into my narrow tract, affording me the opportunity to make a memorable scene that I can leak to *Entertainment Tonight*.

Flight attendant, didn't I hear there's a flab limit per passenger now? Why isn't this mastodon paying for two seats? I have an aisle seat. There is no one in the middle. I have nothing to bitch about. My feelings are mixed. Nothing is pure, I wrote about *East of Eden* after a festival of Steinbeck's books-into-movies in the late '80s, which I left renewed, with almost boyish confidence in my ideals, what I could do that others before me could not—of course could not, they were not me! I could define filmic art the way Lionel Trilling and Alfred Kazan had defined modern literature! "Nothing is pure, but the film version of this novel brings us a confluence of words. With actors, screenwriter, director, cinematographer, editor, composer that overwhelmed me anew by the complexity, the Aristotelian tractability of life made into art about life intractable." And, yes, I can quote myself by heart if I have written it down.

Celebrity! From the Latin "to celebrate," as in: We celebrate them for no reason on earth other than our own pathetic lack of substance. "You resent the wealth of the people you review," Stallone accused me following my review of the unspeakable *Rambo: First Blood Part II* (1985). So withering—and accurate—was my appraisal that it remains a film school staple, trotted out in countless film analysis classesthe world over as "a perfect example," as one lily white professor at the University of Utah once wrote, "of calling a spade a spade."

Yes, Sylvester, I resent your wealth, your celebrity, your promiscuity, and your unearned political standing, but none of that has anything to do with the fact that you're an execrable actor in an excremental movie. I had written: "The deceit in the conceit of an American avenger with steroid pecks, lathered in olive oil, wearing an undulating pubic wig, revising the abject failure of my nation in Vietnam made me laugh, made me sick. The actor wrote the script himself. For himself. It is a masturbatory exegesis on post-Vietnam American male impotence." The review was the first time the *Daily News* had used symbols in its pages to mask someone's use of a perceived profanity. The closing sentence of my review: "Shame on the egregious makers of this propagandist, populist s***. We lost a war we should have won when we actually fought it." My editor urged me to change "shit" to "excrement," a variant on excremental, which I had used above, but I insisted that was too polite a word and that I would accept the "s" followed by three asterisks. I realized at some point—an incremental understanding—that I despised the male of the species and that there was no word for it. There is misanthropy and misogyny for hatred of mankind and of women, but nothing to denote one's loathing of men, per se. Manthropy lacks the musicality of the other two.

In the early eighties, I was feminized by Cassandra Rosenblum DeBoom and began to *write* respectfully of women. Streep, MacLaine, Pfeiffer. Even a kind piece after

The Witches of Eastwick about Cher Bono, though I couldn't *resist* a riff on her competition with Michael Jackson in the torture of the flesh department. I was the first to point out that Nicole Kidman had the talent to be way more than the girlfriend of the modestly talented, big of nose and small of stature Tom Cruise. Cass loved Cruise and thought less of Kidman, accusing me of favoring Kidman because she was the doppelganger of the six-foot, linear, curly-haired, monster-forehanded Maxine Abigail DeBoom. Directors, producers, studio executives (virtually all men in my formative years) hated me for my perceived bias against their gender (and the gender virtually always at the center of their movies). I gained vigor from their united enmity. My paper and network were threatened over the years with 162 lawsuits for libel (spoken) and slander (written). None ever went to trial. And none was settled out of court with cash. Only twice did people come after me physically. In the first case—Bruce Willis—a gaggle of bodyguards intervened before I squashed his nuts into canned peas. In the second case, I slammed Brian DePalma (whom I had decreed the worst director of the half century, either half), into an upholstered easy chair at a crowded Bar Mitzvah reception and told him I'd rip out his leftover hair, follicle by follicle, if he said one more pompous, self-serving, historically inaccurate word about his place in the canon of moving pictures. This incompetence had just razed Tom Wolfe's *Bonfire of the Vanities* (a book I admired and had said so, adding in the finale of the piece that Wolfe was the only writer I considered as intelligently acerbic as I, calling down a torrent of offended blather from the proletariat and snarly rebuke from lovers of the vituperative John Simon). A while ago.

Migdalia Cruz

excerpts from

Dreams of Home

from

The Best American
Short Plays 1991–1992

PEDRO   I am so afraid at night. I cry sometimes. I cry
thinkin' my eyes might close and I might fall asleep and
wake up in the dark, by myself. I pray to Mary that I don't.
I talk to Jesus when I am almost sleeping in the dark and he
keeps me up. I stay up for a chat with the only begotten son.
He knows how it is. He knows how important it is to stay
awake. Things happen when you sleep. Your clothes
disappear and you freeze. People touch you and stare.
You gotta put on as many clothes as you can in case you
nap and somebody tries to get you naked. A man don't let
people see him naked in the street. That's weak. That's no
good. He gets put someplace or somebody sucks on him.
That's weak. You gotta suck first. You gotta look for people
to suck on. That's why you got lips. That's why your nose
fills up with dirt and you gotta breathe through your

mouth...so you learn how to suck. Another thing I do is
bite my fingers. That's how I know it's almost nighttime.
I try to stay in the light, on a street corner, or in a building
where rich people live...rich people always got lights.
And they make loud noises at night. They grind their
teeth together and it keeps me up. It's the same as biting
my own fingers.

[*Pause.*]

It hurts the same too. That's the only bad thing—but I don't
need to sleep that much anyway. Not like some people. Some
people get their feet beat on by people. And people shake
their umbrellas in the sleeping people's faces and throw empty
beer cans at them. That's the worst because they're empty.
Who wants that? But you can make five cents. Unless it hit
you just right—and then it just bounce away from you onto
the tracks. And then it's good-bye. But I'm smarter than that.
I stay awake. I sleep with one eye all the way open, like the
Indians. I got Indian in me. I hold my liquor like an Indian-
like this...

[*He holds a pint of rum between his two hands like he's praying.*]

Like a gift from God.

[*He hits the floor with his palms like he's playing the congas as the
lights fade.*]

• • • •

PEDRO   I used to be afraid of the dark. I would fight to keep it away. Stand under bright lights and pray for morning...but I couldn't keep it away forever. One day I decided to let it in, to feel the darkness creeping under my nails, into my mouth, through my hair. It was so comfortable there, I thought it would never move. It was just the right place for it...so I made friends...with the dark. I said welcome and it stayed awhile. It brought some of its friends to nest inside me. Friends with six legs, the four-legged ones came and slept in my pockets. I was not alone in the dark anymore. Life scratched and buzzed and cracked and squeaked all around me. We grew so close. I could tell what they were feeling. A bite on my left arm—hunger—a bite on my right arm—love. I got them figured out. Right now they're both—hungry and in love. Like me. This woman I got lying near me. She's the same.

[*Pause.*]

Maybe I can catch us something to eat. Maybe I can cook us dinner. We can have a date and dance together. And when we crawl in between the sheets, maybe we'll be alone. That's how you know it's true love—you crawl in together and don't remember nothing else and when you're done doing it, you think about each other's face and you rock together and hold each other and feel safe—not excited or tired or proud—just safer than you ever felt before. Safe without locks or guns or money. Safe in the dark because nobody can tell you you're not where you want to be because nobody can see where you are.

Murray Schisgal

excerpt from

The Man Who Couldn't Stop Crying

from

The Best American Short Plays 1997–1998

MARCELLO   [*Overwrought.*] Wait! Wait! Don't ring for the elevator, sweetheart. Please. Two minutes, that's all I ask. Darling, I am going to change. There's no question about it. One can change. One has choices, free will. Throughout history we have examples...

[*Horrified.*]

No, don't! Don't ring for the elevator. I am changing, sweetheart. The process has already begun. Aren't you aware of it? Haven't you noticed? I'm not crying! Do you see me crying? I have no desire to cry. There's nothing to cry about. I *am* relatively young and healthy and well-off. And I'm happy! Yes, yes, I can say it without embarrassment, I am genuinely happy! Would you like to hear me laugh, darling? I can...

[*Horrified.*]

Why did you press the elevator button? Don't go, not yet. Sweetheart, look at me. Listen to me. I'm laughing. I am laughing. This is not fake.

[*He feigns several varieties of hearty laughter.*]

Did you hear me laughing? Did you? It's not fake. It felt wonderful! I thought I'd never be able to laugh again! But I did laugh. I did. And I am happy, honey, and I love life and I love you, darling. More than anything in the world. And, please, please, let me apologize for saying before that you sounded masculine. How stupid of me! You are definitely not masculine. You are feminine, totally and completely! You are so feminine, it frightens me, it...Where...? Where are you going?

[*Horrified.*]

No, don't walk into the elevator! Don't leave without me! Wait, I'll get my jacket! Pam!

[*Offstage, the elevator carries* PAMELA *down to the lobby. Quickly,* MARCELLO *takes off bathrobe, tosses it aside, gets jacket from the closet, puts it on, hurries to rear window, where he pulls up linen shade and opens window. During the above,* MARCELLO *performs a finger-snapping, shuffling step as he sing-songs what follows.*]

I am happy. And I am glad, I am laughing 'cause I'm not sad. Life is good. Life is great. Now is the time to celebrate.

[*He stops his sing-song step and feigns several laughs before leaning out of open window; shouts:*]

Pam! Here, up here! I'll meet you at the Stanhope! I'll be there in a few minutes! Okay? Love you!

[*He closes window, and resumes his finger-snapping, shuffling step as he sing-songs what follows.*]

I can't be sad,
I must be glad
To have a life
And a loving wife.

[*He stops his sing-song step and feigns riotous laughter as he exits, slamming door shut behind him.*]

Ronald Ribman

excerpt from

The Cannibal Masque

from

The Best American
Short Plays 1994–1995

What good's your marks if you can't buy anything with them.
Now with American cigarettes a good smoke is always a good
smoke, and with people who gotta have them—who can tell?

[*Turning the cigarette pack over and over on the table.*]

Made a nice friend for myself up in Hamburg last
week…shop girl, wedding ring on her finger. She sees me
smoking one of my cigarettes in a bakery and comes over and
wants to buy them. When I tell her I ain't interested in selling
them for money, she gets the drift of what I want and starts
offering me certain favors in exchange for a carton. That's
when I hit her with it. "I ain't got a carton, lady, all I got's a
pack." Now you may think that was a pretty good deal, her

for a lousy carton of cigarettes, but I could see she was a real smoker and I could tell she was really hurting. You know how some people get when they're really hurting for a cigarette.

[*Deeply inhaling and blowing the smoke out.*]

I figured the longer I dragged things out, the more I could cut the price down. So I just sat there at the table with her, talking, drinking my coffee, eating a stack of those Linzertortes they make up there with the raspberry jam coming out, and all the time pushing around the pack so she could keep her eyes on it. [...] Sure I could of, but that would've been missing the beauty part of it, you see, seeing her squirm. That's just the way I am. So now she's down to a pack, so I say, "Fifteen." For five minutes she's laughing in my face about how she ain't gonna go with me for no fifteen cigarettes, so now I tell her I ain't offering fifteen cigarettes no more. Now I'm offering five, on account of her wasting my time and making me late on my deliveries. She just sits there looking at me like I was crazy, and I'm taking my hi-ho time sucking in smoke, enjoying myself, watching the expression on her face, knowing I got all the cards in the deck because she's hurting for a smoke and I don't really give a shit. Hell, why should I, with those black circles under her eyes, her lips all cracked, and her nails discolored and broken by the famine? Well, the long and the short of it is...and this is the real beauty part of it...you wanna know what I got her for? A cigarette. One lousy cigarette! After we finished, she's sitting there on the edge of the bed with her hands hanging down between her legs and the smoke coming up from the cigarette, telling me how I've degraded her by buying her for a single cigarette, and how it wouldn't have been so degrading if I had just given her a carton, or at least a pack. What the hell? Why should anybody give more than they have to? Besides, if you're gonna sell yourself for smoke, how is a carton less degrading than one? People sure got crazy ideas about what it takes to humiliate themselves.

[*Shouting toward the kitchen.*]

Let's go with that pork! I don't have all day! [...] Now you take a guy like you. Soon as we started talking, I could tell you had too much class to humiliate yourself over anything, no matter how bad you wanted it. Guys like you would rather croak than come out and ask for it...not that asking would do you any good, if you get my drift, because that's just the way I am.

[*Putting away the pack of cigarettes.*]

Zilvinas Jonusas

excerpt from

The Cleaning

from

The Best American
Short Plays 2006–2007

JOSEF K. Then why am I constantly reminded that I'm not fit to live, that I'm a sick person, that God will punish me for my…Leni…I already knew from a very young age that there is something in me I won't be able to change. I knew it from the very first time I saw a naked man and had that strange feeling.…It happened on the beach when I was twelve. Every summer my mother, my brother, and I would go and spend our days there. One day I had the urge to go and look around. After I wandered away from my mother and my brother I found myself in the dunes with naked men lying all around me. The excitement of seeing those men took over me and I sat on a bench and started looking at them. A guy as old as I am now approached me. He sat down on the bench next to me. He pointed to one of the older men on the dunes and said: "This man is not a good man. You should not listen what he says to you." And right after that he asked me if he could suck my pee-pee. It sounded very strange to me, but it was exactly what I wanted to hear at that moment. When I heard those words, I thought that all the water from my body had evaporated. My mouth was dry as the Sahara Desert. After a moment of trying to say something, I just nodded, and followed him to the dunes to have what I wanted to have. Time stopped then. Later I regretted what I did. I heard that it was wrong and that it's a deadly sin to have sex with men. But, surprisingly, at that moment it was so right that I completely forgot about time. I remember how we got undressed, I remember the guy asking me if I had done this before. Even though that was my very first time I knew what to do with the guy.... I remember how the guy came. I remember how suddenly I realized that my mother and my brother were probably looking for me. Without even saying a word I jumped into my shorts and ran to the sea to wash off all that excitement and guilt. My throat was even dryer. I tried to wash it down with the salty sea water, but it just got worse.... God, I'm so thirsty.

[*The sound of pouring water into a glass is heard.*]

I saw my brother looking at me with a strange look as if he had seen me with that man. Later I realized that he actually did see me going after the man to the dunes.... He just kept saying: "This man is bad. This man is bad." From that day on, I was secretly visiting the same beach area (I could not

stop myself from going there as often as I could.) Even if
nothing would happen, I needed to see them. Every time after
I would finish with one man or another I would run into the
water to wash that something which was unwashable. Every
time I would go home with that feeling that everybody knew
what I was doing. . . . I had to hide myself inside a thick shell. I
dived into studying and sports. I made myself busy all the
time just to forget who I really am. The strange thing was
that in the meantime I still was able to fall in love with girls. I
thought that I am (was) "normal." But somehow I never
wanted to touch a woman's body the way I liked to touch a
man's. Somehow I never felt with a woman as close as I was
with another man. The real understanding of a man's love
came to me much later. It came after I met you, Leni. I
remember that day. You were leaning next to a wall and were
wearing exactly the same outfit as you are wearing right now.
You were beaming that strange light which attracts men as
bees to the honey. You approached me and asked if I would be
interested in having a glass of champagne with you later. I
said yes, and our evening finished in somebody's house. Even
though we were sleeping completely dressed, my fingers were
able to feel your wet desire. I believe we kissed each other the
whole night. Then we had another "glass of champagne"
night. I remember feeling my body erect for such a long time,
that it was hurting me beyond words. But it was different.
Something really important was missing. Later on I learned
about your child. I really felt grown up then, even though I

was only twenty-one at the time. I was already thinking about what a good father I could be to him.... One evening you introduced me to your best friend. That was when my whole life went crashing down on me, because I was thinking of getting married to you, but after that night...I had a rum with your best friend and realized that drinking champagne with you was just an image I wanted to have. Leni, my reality was rum, not champagne. I know you are probably disgusted by me right now, but your friend was who I wanted to be with for the rest of my life.

Clay McLeod Chapman

birdfeeder

from

The Best American Short Plays 2007–2008

one of five monologues collected by
Daniel Gallant under the heading
Five Story Walkup

Wasn't until winter when word finally got around about
Michael, a group of hunters discovering his body about three
miles into the woods. First day of deer hunting season usually
brings back a month's worth of venison stretched along the
front hood of every Chevrolet in town—only this year, most
trucks came back bare, their empty fenders still caked in a
crust of dried blood from last season's kill. Looked that way,
at least. Maybe it was just rust. Instead of heading to Sally's
Tavern, where everyone parks their cars to compare their
quarry, seeing who has the citation, who brought back the
biggest buck, sneaking their beers out into the parking lot
even though they know it's against the law, Sally turning a
blind eye to her customers as they buy their beer and duck

out the door again—this afternoon, first day of deer hunting
season—most men just rushed right over to Sheriff Flaherty's
office on their own, as sober as a bunch of newborn babies,
leading him and a handful of his officers up Route 2, right
where the highway lines up alongside the woods, nothing but
miles and miles worth of trees, parking their trucks in the
ditch just next to the road and cutting through the forest.
Heading right to Michael. They say it was John Whalthorne
who found him. He'd been following this buck for about a
half mile, keeping his distance until he knew he had a clear
shot—his eyes wandering through the woods by way of the
scope attached to his rifle—only to catch some color in his
crosshairs, this flash of blue. Turns out to be Michael's Levi's.
The weather had washed the brightness out, months' worth
of rain rinsing the dye away—his favorite pair of pants having
faded into this phantom hue. This baby, baby blue. His bones
were nothing but wind chimes now, knocking up against each
other in the breeze. Birds had begun to take him away, one
peck at a time—plucking what pieces of him they could pull
free with their beaks, bit by bit. He looked like a birdfeeder
up there, hanging from that branch. Everyone knows the
woods is where you go when you want to keep a secret. The
deeper into these trees you reach, the darker the secret you
want to keep. Only secrets I've ever kept are of Michael. He'd
lay a leaf against my chest, watching it rise and fall with every
breath—the frond mimicking my rib cage, only smaller, as if
it were two chests pressed against each other. His breath

always tasted of cigarettes, like dried leaves at the back of his mouth. My father always thought the two of us were sneaking off into the woods to have ourselves a smoke, smelling cigarettes on my breath every time I'd come home—but the funny thing was, I never had a cigarette in all of my life. Only Michael. We'd make our way to this clearing in the trees, taking the entire day just to walk there—hiking farther and farther into the forest, until there was nothing around us. Nothing at all. Not the hum of a truck, not the whir of some lawn mower. Not another human being for miles. We'd lay on our backs, slipping out of our T-shirts—feeling what sun could make its way through the trees, these specks of light resting themselves on our chests. That's where I'd kiss him, letting every patch of light lead my lips across his body—as if the sun were saying, Kiss him there. And—Kiss him there. Thinking about Michael out there, all winter. Hanging by that branch, the tension in his neck relenting more and more. Thinking about his body breaking down, changing colors. Shifting pigments. Thinking about all those birds swooping down, pecking at his neck. Tugging on his lips as if they were earthworms. Taking away what they could carry back to their babies, dangling his lips over their beaks, feeding his kisses to their family. You know, it wouldn't have been far off for people to believe Michael had run away, having done it a couple times already. Only difference is, he'd always come back. Whether it was a few hours or a day on the road, Michael would always make his way home. So when it reached a week, his mother started to worry. Like really worry. But by then Michael was already in the woods, slowly disappearing—trying to hide himself inside the stomachs of every animal willing to nibble on him. Thinking—*Nobody would ever look for me in here.* Thinking—*It's safer inside these stomachs.* The weather and elements had decimated the rest of his clothes, chewing through his T-shirt until it was nothing but scraps of fabric. You couldn't even recognize the Metallica decal ironed along the front. The e and the t were just about the only letters left. The others had peeled free, flaking off into the air. I was there when he bought that shirt, wearing it to school the very next day. I remember how firm it felt when it was new, like cardboard, the cotton starting off all stiff, the creases in its sleeves keeping crisp for weeks—before it finally descend into its tenderness. He loved that shirt. He would pull it off and place it under my head, as a pillow—the two of us resting on the ground, looking up at the sky just above us, a few stars hanging over our heads, the trees blocking out the rest, braided by branches, as if I'd put both of my hands right over my face, a latticework of fingers hiding the sky from my eyes. We'd spend the night out in the woods, telling our parents that we were sleeping over at each other's house. Holding him, I remember listening to the trees warping over our heads, every bending branch making this squealing sound in the dark—until it almost sounded like my arms were bending as well, the weight of Michael in my grip causing my limbs to twist. *What if someone finds out about us? What do we do then? Don't worry*, he said. *We're safe out here.* He was wearing those blue jeans the last time I saw him, nearly six months ago now. Pretty much wore those pants every day of his life, anyhow—but I know it was when we were together last, when I last laid eyes on him, that I was the last person to see him alive. Because there was no note, no cry for help. Just his body breaking down. People keep asking me why. *Why would he head out into the woods alone and hang himself, waiting out there all winter for someone to find him?* Suddenly I'm an authority on his unhappiness? I'm the expert on what makes him tick? Even Michael's mother's come to me, desperate for some sense of closure, just so she won't have to blame herself for what happened. *You were his best friend, Sean. He would've talked to you about these things.... Did he ever mention depression? Did he ever say anything about suicide?* I knew he was out there. When Michael first disappeared, I went out into the woods by myself—going to the only place where I felt safe, where I could be alone. And that's when I saw him, swaying. His head bowed against his chest. It was better for someone else to find him. Someone other than me. If I'd been the one to take Sheriff Flaherty out into the woods, other questions would get asked. Questions like: *What were you doing out there in the first place? What were you two boys doing so far out in the forest, alone?* Questions like that don't stop themselves from getting asked, even if you provide an answer. In a town as small as this, sometimes—the answer isn't what people are after. Sometimes they want your secrets. That's what frightened

Michael more than anything. That's what sent him out into the woods by himself. Sometimes, saying your lips are sealed isn't enough. The best way to keep a secret is to cinch your throat shut, cutting off the air that cushions your deepest, darkest truths. Deer hunting season would come in a few months, only for someone to stumble upon him. They'd rush back for Sheriff Flaherty, dragging him through the woods, cutting Michael's body down. Doing it properly. Until then, I'd know where I could find him. I'd know where he'd be. I've kept him secret for six months now, never mentioning Michael to anyone—because there are more secrets where that came from. More than I can count.

I keep his eyes, as blue as his jeans. I keep his lips, as thin as earthworms. I keep the taste of his mouth out in those woods. Nobody knows about him and me out here.

Daniel Frederick Levin

A Glorious Evening

from

The Best American
Short Plays 2007–2008

one of five monologues collected by
Daniel Gallant under the heading
Five Story Walkup

[HARRY *is sitting at a table with a flower on it, looking out at the audience. The level of realism for the following is low, particularly for processes that occur: Delivery should be understated, acted with restraint, with only perhaps a hint of emotion at the end.*]

HARRY [*Pause.*] I'm really looking forward to tonight. How are you feeling…are you cold? Good.…It was really beautiful out tonight, wasn't it? Did you notice there was like a sweet smell in the air when you were coming here? And a good sweet smell, not a bad sweet smell that you don't know where it's coming from. A good sweet smell, I don't know, it's probably some early flowers, some mulch thawing out, a little wood, probably some sulfates. God, you look…So, my cell phone is off, computer off, Blackberry, don't have one. The

TV is sleeping for the night, the radio...the radio, maybe a faroff wisp of a jazz song, if anything. But thank God those are all inventions. Thank God we don't really need any of those things. Thank God all we need is...this. I made a few, eh-em, improvements.

[*Indicating flower.*]

There's one of these on the bathtub ledge, for the bath before we...didn't draw the water yet. I didn't want it to get cold. But I figure that's maybe when we can listen to that jazz, you know? Is there anything better than listening to jazz against running water? And we'll find a station with not that many instruments. Just maybe a saxophone...and a bass...just that. No piano. We don't need piano.

[*Smiles.*]

I love you. Are you sure you're not cold? Hot? I can open the window more.

[*Realizing something.*]

You know what? I think I forgot to brush my teeth. I'm...do you need anything? Okay.

[HARRY *makes tooth-brushing motion, not that realistic.*]

I'm brushing my teeth. I'm brushing my teeth. I'm brushing my teeth. I'm brushing my teeth. I'm brushing my teeth. I'm

brushing my teeth. I'm brushing my tongue. I'm spitting. I'm
rinsing. I'm back. Hi. Did I miss much?

[*Pause.*]

I have plenty of protection. And it's the gentle kind.
Everything is taken care of. There's nothing at all to worry
about.

[*He breathes.*]

What a glorious night. Temperature is right. Smell is right.
Sound is good. Vision is wonderful. Touch will be amazing.
Taste will be...pretty good, well worth it. Well worth it.
Smell. Sound. Sight. Touch. Taste. Smell. Sound. Sight.
Touch. Taste. Smell. Sound...I need just one sec. Will you
be all right for a sec? Excuse me. [*He pauses. Stands up.*] I'm
using the bathroom, I'm using the bathroom, I'm using the
bathroom, I'm using the bathroom, I'm using the bathroom,
I'm using...[*Pause.*] I'm using the bathroom the other way,
I'm using the bathroom, I'm reaching for the switch, I'm
using the bathroom, I'm using the bathroom, I'm trying to be
quiet, I'm using the bathroom, I'm using the bathroom, I'm
using the bathroom, I'm using the bathroom, I'm looking for
matches, I'm using the bathroom, I'm using the bathroom, I'm
using the bathroom, I'm using the bathroom, I'm finishing
up, I'm finishing, I think, I'm ripping off paper....I'm ripping
off again, and ripping off again...and again...and again...

and I think I'm finished...and I'm finished...and I'm finished, I'm done. Hi. Sorry about that. Now I just feel... perfect. Are you feeling all right?

[*Rapid fire.*]

Cold hot bored wired up down shy bold deaf blind stifled? Y'sure?

[*Sighs.*]

It's such a beautiful evening. There's this mood...this...well, it's the jazz...it's...

[*Noticing something.*]

I'm having a little trouble swallowing. I'm having trouble swallowing. I'm having trouble swallowing. It's like choking, but I can breathe. I'm having trouble swallowing.

[*Louder.*]

I'm having trouble swallowing! It passed.

[*He breathes for a moment.*]

I was saying, swallow, it's like the jazz, best on an, swallow, old record, swallow again, I'm thinking about swallowing, I'm thinking about swallowing, I'm thinking about swallowing, I feel hot. Are you Okay? I have a little more saliva. It seems to have passed. It seems to have passed.

[*He sighs again.*]

What a beautiful... I just can't wait. I can't wait for later. I want to first draw that bath. Then I want to go to the bathroom. I want to swallow. I want to be quiet. I want to fantasize. I want to do everything... I want to feel intense, intense pleasure. I'm so excited, you know? Would you mind leaving? Right now? It's really beautiful out. You'll get to smell that sweet smell. Remember? The mulch? Now. Go on. Leave. Go on. Get out of here. Get out of here. Get out!

[*Bringing himself under control and retreating back.*]

Swallow.
Breathe.
Swallow.
Breathe.
I'm imagining.
I'm breathing.
I'm really looking forward to tonight.

Murray Schisgal

The Artist and the Model

from

The Best American
Short Plays 1994–1995

characters

BROMBERG is in his late sixties. But he is a vigorous man, with little slackness; his eyes burn with a fierce, truculent intensity. And yet he is old; his hair is in need of a haircut, his face a shave, his nails a brushing. Oddly, he seems to be in a great hurry, poised for movement.

ANGELICA is a non-speaking participant, not particularly attractive. Nor unattractive. She is Latino or Mediterranean. She is in her twenties or early thirties, with a strong, solid, full-breasted body. Her abundant flesh fairly bursts with her naked womanhood. The role requires a professional model. Her actions are prompted by three considerations: (1) she needs the job; (2) she is acutely aware of BROMBERG's age and isolation; (3) she is in awe of his talent, his ability to create beautiful things.

scene

BROMBERG's studio in Tribeca.

time

1994. Winter. Twenty-two minutes after eight o'clock in the morning.

[*Lights.* BROMBERG *is seated on a paint-encrusted, white, straight-backed kitchen chair of the forties, downstage, right; his large, veined hands rest on his knees; between his knees is a darkly varnished cane. A rectangular sketchpad leans against the downstage leg of the chair. Farther to the right upstage is a plant stand on which there is a potted plant, leafy and vibrantly green. A tin watering can is on the floor beside it. On the left, mid-stage, is a model's platform covered with a worn faded oriental carpet. If there is any discernible expression on* BROMBERG's *face, it is one of displeasure, if not anger. He wears slightly paint-splattered, baggy white housepainter's pants; heavily paint-splattered, ankle-high work shoes; a bleached, clean, pressed denim shirt with sleeves rolled above his elbows—sticks of charcoal, pens, and pencils protrude from his shirt's breast pocket. Shortly* ANGELICA *enters. She is late. She*

*has been running. She tries to repress the sound of her breathlessness.
She removes, quickly, her coat, scarf, knitted cap. It is cold out, al-
though a bright sun shines through the unseen skylight. BROM-
BERG's eyes hold fast to her. He clenches his jaw to prevent himself
from speaking. ANGELICA throws her things on an ancient,
brown, wicker chair that is left, angled towards platform. A vintage
paisley shawl lies across the armchair. Without a pause, ANGELI-
CA removes her street shoes, skirt, cardigan sweater, blouse, white
athletic socks, pantyhose, bra, and panties; all are thrown on the armchair or, inadvertently, on the floor. A salvaged wooden box with a
dozen or so art books on it is at the side of the armchair, downstage.
As soon as she's undressed, she steps up on the platform, waits to receive instructions. She is unable to return BROMBERG's fixed,
obtrusive stare. She invariably turns away from him to look down at
the carpet or across at a wall or at whatever object affords her refuge.
Initially BROMBERG's voice is a low-spoken growl, a mumble, a
muttering of words.*]

BROMBERG   If you remember...when I first retained you
to model for me...months ago...I asked if it was possible for
you to be here at six o'clock in the morning...since I get up
at five o'clock in the morning and by six o'clock in the
morning I am anxious to start my work.

[*A pause.*]

You answered by saying it would be impossible for you to
arrive before eight o'clock in the morning because...you had

to take the subway from your apartment in the Bronx...down to my studio. You said you were afraid to ride the subway so early in the morning.

[*A pause.* ANGELICA *stands on the platform. Shortly she will instinctively lower her hands in front of her pubic hair.*]

I said you could work for me if you arrived here promptly at eight o'clock in the morning; no later; promptly at eight o'clock in the morning. On those days I required...your services. You agreed. You agreed knowing full well that when I'm scheduled to work with you...I am incapable of doing any other work until you arrive. That means from the hour of six o'clock in the morning until...eight o'clock in the morning...I am waiting...I am waiting for you to arrive.

[*A pause. He breathes audibly, as if he has exhausted himself; yet his voice becomes more didactic, firm, angry.*]

I don't imagine you have any idea what that's like. To wait...two hours...two whole hours. Substantive. Time. When the body and mind are...energized...poised to grapple and do battle with the...the illusive. In-val-u-able hours that can never be...captured, recycled, like soda bottles, beer cans...yesterday's garbage.

[*A pause.* ANGELICA *folds her arms across her chest; she is cold.*]

I imagine that at six o'clock in the morning you're still

wrapped in your boyfriend's arms...without a care or
frustrated bone in your body. While I wait...to work...to fill
my lungs with mouthfuls of fresh air, oxygen, to be able
to...to breathe.

[*A pause.*]

I believe I told you on more than one occasion that when I
am not working...I have difficulty...breathing. This
difficulty increases the longer I am unable to work. Tension
builds. My heart...palpitates, a-rhyth-mic-a-lly. My
abdominal muscles...cramp. My lungs feel like they're...co-
llap-sing. I have to work so I can breathe. So I won't die...of
suff-o-ca-tion.

[*A pause. He rises, walks to the rear right, leaning on his cane; his
disabled leg is stiff, as if tied to a board; he moves it along, not with
pain or excessive effort. He stands at rear and looks through an unseen wall window. During the above,* ANGELICA *runs to armchair, grabs her thigh-length cardigan sweater, puts it on, buttons it,
and returns to stand on platform.*]

Two hours and twenty-two minutes I waited for you this
morning. An intolerable amount of time. For someone who
is...suffocating. I would send you home, right now! This
minute! If I could replace you, find someone else, anyone
else, immediately, without delay, so I could work. Finally.

[*A pause.*]

But since I can't on such short notice...and since I refuse to waste any more time with this...this rubbish! Be advised that this is the last day of your employment with me. Be so advised. When you leave these premises at the end of the day, I do not wish to see you again.

[*A pause. He walks to plant stand, picks up watering can and waters plant. His voice is a soft, controlled drone, with specified pauses, words frequently spoken reflectively to himself.*]

I want you out of my life. Once and for all. I have no need of this...agitation. I'll get someone in here who's prompt and appreciative and who is a little more fastidious in her *toilette*. A woman of some class, sophistication. I won't have to listen to your endless whining, the endless gossip I've been subjected to. Relentlessly. Relentlessly. No more late-night horror stories about your...liaisons, your...debaucheries, your Peter, Peter, Richie, Richie, your hordes of former employers! That...That grubby second-rate poseur Ostrovski, that no talent, minusculist *pissoir*, Magenetti, your pathetic pap-art petomane, Wilberquist. Work for them, why don't you?

[*He turns to her.*]

They're begging you to go back to them, aren't they? How many times have they phoned you, written to you, waited on your doorstep for you to come home at two, three in the morning!

[*Mimics sarcastically.*]

Oh, please, my sweet, dear Angelica, please, come back and pose for me! Leave that monster Bromberg, that old, demented, loathsome, egomaniacal cripple! I beg you, Angelica. I can't paint without you, Angelica. I can't create without you, Angelica. You're the best, the most beautiful, the most desirable model in the whole...

[*Suddenly explodes, wagging cane.*]

Go! Get out of here! To hell with you! I can't work today. You've made it impossible! Out! Out! I want you out of here!

[ANGELICA *moves to armchair, finds her panties amidst pile of clothes. As she's about to put them on,* BROMBERG *shakes his head, eyes tightly closed; quietly.*]

No.

[*A pause.*]

No. No.

[*Anguished.*]

I... I can't afford to... waste... anymore... time.

[*Shakes his head.*]

I can't.

[ANGELICA *stares at him.* BROMBERG *opens his eyes. A breath. Firmly.*]

Stay. I have to get something done, something...started. For today. Just today. Finish your work. You'll be paid.

[ANGELICA *places her panties in cardigan sweater's pocket, takes off sweater, steps on platform and assumes pose #1: one that says I have no ill will towards you; I want to help you draw something beautiful.* BROMBERG *sits on kitchen chair, lays cane on floor; he picks up sketchpad, places it on his lap, turns pages, examining previous drawings—none of them pleases him. He finds a clean page, takes charcoal from shirt pocket and begins sketching* ANGELICA. *Now and then we hear the stick of charcoal scratching across the sheet of paper.* BROMBERG *is content. His breathing comes naturally. In a moment he appraises his sketch. He is dissatisfied with it. He turns the page and starts again. A smile breaks on his face.*]

So who is it this week? Peter or Richie? Did your mother convince you that an unemployed gas-station attendant is preferable to an apprentice butcher? No gossip today? No little tidbits of blue-collar erotica? How about your girlfriend Gloria? Is she having the baby or has the notorious gigolo, Alphonso the Barber, persuaded her that an aborted fetus is next to Godliness? What about your cousin, the disco king? Did he test positive? Did he ever discover the culprit of his concern?

[*He sketches a bit.*]

You poor young people nowadays. You don't know how pathetic you all are. Scrounging in the garbage dumps for momentary pleasures. In a rotting city. A rotting country. Second-rate. Sliding inexorably into mediocrity. The land of no-more opportunity. Shrinking horizons. Guns and condoms hanging from the gnarled, yellow beak of a bald-headed eagle. America, America, thou hast seen thy day of glory and now lie barren and desiccated under the cold, barren sun.

[*Concentrates on sketch for a bit.*]

I don't imagine in your vast reading of American history you learned that there was such a thing in the early forties as a World War designated numero duo. It was thanks to that effort of moralistic futility that I'm compelled to drag this warped leg about like a superfluous erection. Oh, don't tax your fragile psyche and try to make sense of this. It was an event of no consequence. An irony. A glitch. God, to have lived to see how it all turned out. Where it ended. Where we are today and what it was like then. Poor bastards. Lambs led to the slaughter. Parades and Dole pineapple juice. Poor, poor bastards.

[*A pause.*]

Now here we are, in the cesspool of the nineties, remembering... nothing. An event of no consequence.

[*Sharply.*]

Change pose!

[ANGELICA *assumes pose #2: she's annoyed, doesn't understand why* BROMBERG *is talking so much this morning. Her stance is provocative, seductive, an attempt to get him to concentrate on his work.* BROMBERG *turns page, sketches for a while; we hear the charcoal scratching the page; speaks softly, almost to himself.*]

I remember, once during the war, I was standing alone...in a bar in Tijuana...drinking a Four Roses and ginger ale.

[*He laughs, amused by his sophomoric choice of drink.*]

I was all of eighteen years. I don't know where my friends were, probably in a whorehouse. I don't know why I wasn't with them. I usually was. I remember...looking up from my drink and I saw, sitting beside me, a young woman, no older than myself. We started talking. I said something funny and she laughed. We exchanged stories, experiences, revealed intimate secrets. We had, along the way, a few drinks. We were high but not drunk. Lifted to that height of reality where we were slightly off the ground...and sight and sound were...brilliantly vivid...Incandescent.

[*A pause.*]

What was her name, that young woman in a bar in Tijuana, during the Second World War? I don't know. Her hair was ocher, amber, topaz. Her eyes were made of bits of mica, glittering specks of turquoise. Her mouth...Pale. Pink. Full. Her teeth, her cheeks...I can see her now. I can taste and smell the soft scent of her. The closeness of her.

[*A pause.*]

There was a jukebox. A dance floor. We danced, on that height of reality that was...incandescent. What was her name? I don't know. But I remember the song...we danced to.

[*Quietly, he speak-sings the lyrics, emphatically pronouncing a word here and there; a similar period song may be used.*]

"Just kiss me once, then kiss me...twice, then kiss me...once again, it's been a...long...long...time. Haven't felt like...this...my dear...since can't remember when . . ."

[*Voice fades out; he tries to sketch; gives it up.*]

"When do you have to be back at the base?" I believe she asked me. "Not until tomorrow afternoon," I lied. "Stay with me." Did she say that? Yes. She did. "Stay with me." "I'd like that. Very much," I replied. Oh, yes. Ohhh, yes, yes, yes. I would like that very much. "The bus to San Diego is leaving in a few minutes," she said. "I have to say good-bye to my girlfriends," she said. "I'll meet you on the bus," she said. She moved her face closer to mine; her lips barely a breath away.

"I'll be on the bus," I said, with all the manhood I could muster, getting up and running out...getting on the bus that was jammed to the rafters with sailors and civilians and...

[*A pause; softly.*]

Change pose.

[*Pose #3:* ANGELICA *thinks of herself as* BROMBERG's *young woman in Tijuana; her pose is as lovely and as simple as she can make it.* BROMBERG *turns page, sketches.*]

My heart is beating so fast at this...minute...I feel like a fool. Anyway...inside the bus, I waited for her, to get on, to join me, thinking, sweating, I should get off, I should find her, I should cry out, "Wait! I'm getting off! Excuse me! Excuse me!" But would you believe that the bus was already moving and she wasn't on it and I was traveling to San Diego... without her? Would you believe...that I never saw her again and up until this minute...

[*A sigh.*]

I never told anyone about her. Not wife numero uno, wife numero duo, mistresses and lovers from numero uno to...infinity. I told no one. From fear of embarrassment by the in-con-se-quen-ti-ality of that...innocuous encounter. In Tijuana. Some fifty years ago. During the war to save democracy. What was her name?

[*Shakes his head.*]

I don't know.

[*Sketches; laughs softly.*]

You do think you're living a life. Peter, Peter, Richie, Richie.

[*He laughs.*]

You have no idea. What life could be. What life was. After…After the war. Those who survived. We were in the center of the world. Right here. In this cesspool of a city. There was more happening within blocks of this studio, on canvas, than anywhere else in God's creation. Did you ever hear of a fellow named de Kooning? Pollock? Gorky? Rothko? Smith? Motherwell? My sweet, dear friend, Jimmy Ernst? Of course not! Why should you? You know Oooostrovski! Maaaga-ne-tta! Wilber-petomane-quist! Those fraudulent imitators of neo-moderne bile and excrement!

[*Sharply.*]

Change pose!

[*Pose #4: ANGELICA is quite peeved by BROMBERG's constant assault on her personal life. Her pose is mean-spirited, aggressive, defiant. BROMBERG sees through it; sharply:*]

Change pose!

[*Pose #5. She holds a particularly horrific pose. At once* BROMBERG *responds.*]

Change pose!

[ANGELICA *gives in. Pose #6: a rather ordinary innocuous one.* BROMBERG *turns page, sketches, the charcoal scratching the paper.*]

But then...back then...we were a community. What an endearing word that is. Community. How rich one felt being part of...a...community. Part of a group, a tribe, a band of brigands who congregated...together. Every night partying at the Cedar's or San Remos's or downstairs at Louie's. Every day at our ateliers, showing one another what we were working on, talking about, arguing about it, competing, putting down, raising up, but always respecting what was original, what was right, what was good. That, too, was...together.

[*A pause.*]

In a city. In a country: Of endless opportunities. Burgeoning horizons. Supreme confidence. In the first full flush of being *numero uno.*

[*Sketches awhile.*]

You had to be around in the sixties to know what I'm talking about. Free. Free at last. The pictures that run through my mind are those of naked, flower-haloed young people, celebrating under the crimson-tinted open sky. *Carpe diem.* Of thee I sing.

[*A pause.*]

What an unforgettable decade. So much happened. Was experienced. That's when making love was such a dance. Hedonism unbridled. Love on the run. Orgasm apotheosized. Ohhh, it does the heart wonders to reflect on it.

[*Tone of voice gradually changes.*]

But those are circumstances that young people nowadays have no way of knowing. Believe me, I am sorry for you. Do not mistake my...outspokenness for a lack of compassion. For an expression in insensitivity. I truly pity you young people nowadays. A night of making love carries with it the horrendous onus of mortality. One forbidden excursion is potentially an act of suicide. How horrible the times. Guns and condoms in the gnarled, yellow beak of a bald-headed eagle. Oh, the horror of it all.

[*A pause.*]

I assume you practice safe sex. I assume you have sufficient intelligence to speak frequently on the subject with your

Peter, Peter and Richie, Richie and whoever else you might be temporarily co-habitating with.

[*Firmly.*]

Change pose.

[*Pose #7: the pose is in the main* ANGELICA *"mooning"* BROMBERG. BROMBERG *barks.*]

Change pose!

[*Pose #8: she juts her pelvis out towards him in a whorish pose.* BROMBERG *is intrigued by it; sketches, scratching charcoal on paper.*]

There's so much that's screwed-up nowadays. It's an ideal age to grow old. One doesn't quite regret as much saying good-bye to the slime and disease and bloodletting that's drowning us. I wouldn't have liked, for anything, being old in the sixties, but being old in the nineties is something of a blessing.

[*He smiles with the thought of it.*]

One can stand on the side and observe the pathetic little lives lived by you...people. I often wonder what it is you look forward to, what dreams and fantasies you have, what you believe in that makes all the...horror of it worthwhile. I can't for the life of me imagine what it is. Marriage? Does that still exist for you young people? I understand the divorce rate is above fifty percent and that's not counting the number of husbands and wives who walk out the door, never to be heard from again.

[*A pause.*]

Family? Is that still a viable option? I would think as the years go by there'll be less and less of that. I would think we're witnessing the last vestiges of a worn-out social convention that has overstayed its usefulness. How many single mothers are there nowadays? How many couples live together without benefit of church or state? No, no, family is an impractical goal nowadays. Not very realistic. You'll probably end up with some jerk, you'll have his brats, he'll walk out and some other jerk will probably walk in to take his place.

[*Sharply.*]

Change pose!

[*He stops sketching; stares at* ANGELICA, *fixedly. Pose #9:* AN-GELICA *has had it; she poses indifferently, repeating poses she's done previously, anticipating his call for a changed pose and posing anew even before he commands her to do so.*]

Did you become impatient? Did you move in with somebody already? Richie, Richie? Peter, Peter? Ostrovski? Maganetta?

One of the innumerable suitors who wait on your doorstep every morning? Change pose!

[*Pose #10: a fantastical "in flight" pose, arms flung outwards, one leg raised.*]

What about your mother? The one person I ever heard you say you had feelings for. Did you just leave her with your young sisters? Is that what she deserves from you? Change pose!

[*Pose #11: another far-fetched pose.*]

Change pose!

[*Pose #12: and another.*]

I thought you wanted more out of your life than a pinch on the ass and a quick lay! Change pose!

[*Pose #13: and another.*]

I thought you were interested in making something of yourself, of giving your life value, of...

[ANGELICA *has had enough. Furiously, she moves to armchair, dresses quickly.* BROMBERG *scrambles to pick up his cane; rises, continues, heedlessly.*]

...of becoming a productive, committed, caring human being!

[*Shouts commandingly.*]

Change pose!

[ANGELICA *pays him no mind.* BROMBERG *shouts again.*]

Change pose! Change pose! I thought you had a passion, passion for books, a passion for painting and music and, and beautiful things! Was that all rot you were giving me? Were you lying, deceiving a man who trusted and believed in you? Is that how you treat people? Is that the extent of your humanitarianism?

[*Pants for a beat or two.*]

I did not dismiss you! I did not say you could go! I said you would be paid if you worked until the end of the day! The end of the day! Otherwise you don't get a penny from me! Not a penny! Now get back on there and we'll…we'll continue…we'll…go on…

[*Loudly; in despair.*]

I cannot waste the day! No matter how much I'd enjoy kicking you out of here! I have…my work…to do! I have to…Change pose! Change pose! Change…

[*He swallows huge mouthfuls of air, watches, helplessly, as* ANGELICA *finishes dressing. She picks up her coat, scarf, knitted cap and is about to leave. A whisper.*]

Angelica.

[*She turns to look at him. Softly.*]

Where were you last night? I wanted, very much, to talk to you. I felt... not tired. I took the subway up to your neighborhood and I... From a candy store I phoned you. I thought we'd have a cup of coffee together and... talk together. I spoke to your mother. She said you were out. She didn't know where. So I... I waited, on your doorstep. Until morning. Two... three... in the morning. You didn't show up.

[*Forces a smile.*]

I won't make that mistake again. I had no sleep. For a man my age... that's a great... sacrifice.

[ANGELICA *moves to him. She puts her arms around his waist and hugs him tightly, pressing her head to his chest. BROMBERG, hands are at his sides, one hand holding his cane. ANGELICA raises her face and kisses him on the mouth, long and hard; passionately. BROMBERG doesn't move, doesn't react. ANGELICA backs away from him, her eyes on him. Abruptly, she turns and exits. BROMBERG stands stiffly, his eyes fixed on the offstage door for several beats. Using his cane, he makes his way to stand on the platform, center, facing front. He drops his cane, unbuttons his shirt, takes it off, drops it on top of the cane. He touches his naked chest with outspread hand, runs his hand over his chest, slowly, once, pressing hard, feeling his warm flesh under his fingers. Hands at his sides, he inhales deeply, tasting the oxygen in his lungs. Exhales. He does this once again. Slowly. Deliberately. Clenching the summation of breath in the fibers of his being. Hands at sides, he raises them, slowly, over his head; his fingertips touch. Slowly he brings his hands down to his sides. He does this once again. Each movement felt throughout his body. Lights begin to fade as he continues with his exercises. Hands splayed on his hips, he moves his torso to the left. Then center. Then to the right. Then center. He does this once again. Slowly. Deliberately. He stretches his arms out forward, slowly moves them perpendicular to his body. Etc. Lights fade out.]*

Peter Maloney

Witness

from

The Best American Short Plays 2006–2007

place

Abu Ghraib Prison, Iraq

time

April 2004

[*Sound of metal door slamming very loudly. At same time lights bump up. Shouts of prisoners, dogs barking somewhere.* KASIM *sits on the lower bunk of an iron bed. There is no mattress, only a plywood board.* KASIM *wears an orange jumpsuit. He holds a baseball in one hand and regards it. He opens his mouth wide, as if he wants to take a bite of the baseball. He looks up at us.*]

KASIM It occurs to me...perhaps they thought we *eat* these things. That they thought it is some kind of fruit, and

that we eat it. I could have told them that *this* is not
indigenous to Iraq, that baseballs do not grow on trees here.
And that, in any case, it is not a fruit. But they do not speak
my language. And the translator was not there when they
tried to feed it
to me.

[KASIM *looks at the baseball. He opens his mouth as wide as possible.
He closes his mouth, looks at us.*]

It barely fit into my mouth. They had to break two teeth to
get it in.

[*He opens his mouth wide again, points with a finger to broken teeth
in back.*]

I tried to spit the baseball out, to push it out with my tongue,
but they tied a scarf around my head to hold it in. With the
baseball in my mouth, I could only breathe through my nose.
It was fortunate for me that it was not the season of my
asthma, or I might have suffocated. I was frightened, and I
wanted to tell them about my asthma, but the baseball in my
mouth made it impossible for me to speak. And, in any case,
they would not have understood me. And the translator was
not there. I had expected that they would understand my
language, or, in fact, any language that I might have spoken.
Frankly, I was surprised that language even came into it. I
imagined that, in an encounter of this kind, words would be

unnecessary. I have never seen a baseball game. Except in the movies. I have a video store. Mostly bootlegs my cousin Nouri brings in from Syria. I've got all the latest, man. On Rashid Street, near the copperware market. Perhaps you know it, KVCD Video? No? Perhaps if you are in the neighborhood you can look in on my shop and if I see you again you can tell me if it is still there.

[*He looks at the baseball, remembers, smiling.*]

Field of Dreams. Starring Mr.... Kevin...

[*He brings his arm back, mimes throwing the ball.*]

Costner.

[*Pain in his right shoulder. He sets the baseball down on the bunk bed.*]

I cannot speak about what has happened to me here. Because...I will soon be leaving and...they asked me not to talk about certain things. They said you would not understand. Certain things you would understand and other things you wouldn't. I myself am confused. I was abducted on the day the Americans captured Saddam. I was with my friend Ameen. The news of Saddam's capture had just come over the TV. I closed up my shop and we ran out into the street. The TV in the window we left on so that people outside could watch the events as they unfolded. I had loaned

Ameen my video camera. He was making a film about the
situation here. At the time of the invasion, he had filmed the
falling statues, and now he wanted to film the people's
reaction to the fall of the man himself. The reaction of the
man in the street. We were hurrying along the river in the
direction of the Al-Salam Palace. There were so many
people, all of them shouting, dancing in the streets.
American soldiers sitting atop their Humvees, grinning,
smoking cigarettes. I was so happy to see Saddam go away.
You know he destroyed our country. He humiliated us. I
thank you, President Bush. There was one tank on the street.
Ameen laughs and says, "Hey, it's Clint Eastwood's tank." I
look, and even with my bad English I can make out, stenciled
on the barrel of the big gun: "GO AHEAD, MAKE MY
DAY." I am standing right by the tank. Ameen was taking
pictures of all the action when somebody behind us starts
shooting at the Americans. Fucking Fedayeen. Stupid guys. I
hear the firing and the bullets hitting the tank and I ducked
down. It becomes a kind of instinct. I know those fuckers are
likely to fire grenades next, so I drop to the ground and I
thought, I will roll under the tank. The tank will protect me.
But it's not that easy to roll under a tank. In fact you can't do
it. The . . . things that go around and around the wheels . . .
treads. And anyway now an American soldier has his foot on
my back and his rifle pushing hard behind my ear and he is
screaming at me in English. The tank is shaking and I hear
explosions, and sure enough Clint is firing the big gun in the

direction the shots came from, he doesn't realize that the Fedayeen are gone. They were there and now they're gone. But that doesn't stop Clint from firing on the place they were. I am lying on my stomach with this boot on my back and the barrel of the gun pushing my head into the pavement and then my video camera joins me there on the ground, all the pieces of it clattering into the gutter. Before I know it my hands are tied together behind my back with the plastic laces and I am being pulled up onto my feet. Ameen is up against the tank, another soldier's got him covered. His hands are tied, too, and he has a sandbag over his head. And just before the bag goes over my head I see that not only the Fedayeen are gone, so is the building they were firing from. In fact, the whole neighborhood isn't there anymore, just piles of concrete and clouds of dust. Stupid fucking Fedayeen. They took us in a Humvee, with other guys they rounded up. To Camp Cropper, out near the airport. They put us in a tent. I didn't see Ameen again.

[*He is quiet for a moment, then, suddenly agitated, he stands and, looking up as if to the upper tier of cells, cries out in a loud voice.*]

AMEEN!…DON'T WORRY ABOUT THE FUCKING CAMERA, MAN! I CAN ALWAYS GET ANOTHER CAMERA!

[*He is quiet again.*]

We were in the tent for eight days. Bagged and cuffed. They gave us a can to piss in, but if you had to piss and it wasn't the *time* to piss and there was no one around to cut the cuffs off you.... There were some stinking fucking dishdashas in that tent after eight days, I'll tell you. Eight days of pissing yourself and a clean jumpsuit looks pretty good. That was in December. It was cold. No one in the tent knew why we were there. Somebody in the tent knew some English and he asked the soldiers why we were there. They told us we knew why. But we didn't know. They said they were the ones who ask the questions and if they didn't like the answers they'd send us all to Guantanamo. They kept saying we were going to Guantanamo, that once we were there we'd be wishing we were back here.

I didn't like hearing this shit. I got tired of hearing about Guantanamo. On the day they moved us out of Cropper one of the soldiers said we were going to Guantanamo. I said he could shove Guantanamo up his ass, it was just another fucking prison where they lock up Afghanis and Al Qaeda guys, and what am I doing here, I run a video store! I didn't say it in English, I don't speak English. But this other stupid guy, the one of us who knew a little English, he *translates* for the fucking American! So when they are loading us into the truck to move us out, this soldier who I told to shove Guantanamo up his ass pulls me aside, holds me back. Everybody is in the back of the truck but me, they're packed in, cuffed and bagged, and the soldier is ready to put a bag on my head. But before he does he takes out his wallet and flips through some pictures he keeps in there. There's his mother and his wife or his girlfriend and his kid or his little brother, I don't know, and he finds the picture he's looking for. He puts his hand on my shoulder like we are buddies and he holds out the wallet with the picture for me to see. It's a picture of him in a red and black checked cap. He's holding a rifle, (an ordinary rifle, not the big gun he's carrying now), and tied across the front of his truck is a deer. He's holding on to the horn of this big deer and looking proud of himself.

[*Change of tone, more intimate. It is important to* KASIM *that we know what he thinks about this.*]

Which reminds me. We can't talk about the art of acting without speaking of Mr.....Robert...De Niro.

[*He waits, as if to check if we agree, his eyes darting left and right. He mimes lifting a rifle, sighting down the barrel.*]

The next thing I know I'm in the dark again and being lifted up, and they throw me across the front of the truck and tie me down. The soldiers are laughing and at first I'm not minding being tied down because the truck has been idling for a while and I am suddenly warmer than I have been in over a week. But by the time we are halfway to Abu Ghraib the hood is red fucking hot and the metal is burning me right through my shirt and my pants.

[*He touches his jumpsuit very gingerly with his fingertips around his middle, his thighs.*]

Can you do something for me? Maybe you can get in touch with my family? Tell my wife where I am. That I'm okay. Do you know the Backstreet Boys? My daughter likes the Backstreet Boys. She *loves* them. Especially Nick. She sent away for a picture, but it never came. That's all she wants in this life, she says, is a picture of this Backstreet Boy signed, "To Layla, love Nick." Maybe it came while I'm in here. Five months, man. Five fucking months, and I still don't know what they want from me. *The Deer Hunter.* Yeah. In the middle of the trip here, a sandstorm hit, and I was really glad for the sandbag on my head, which protected me somewhat. When we go there, they untied me, took the bag off, and this...unearthly... unearthly light was everywhere, because of the dust. Everything was...*ghamidh*. You know this word? Mysterious. Ambiguous. Yeah. When we got here we finally could take a shower. They took our clothes away. They took everything away. My watch. The thing is, I wonder if it's really five months, or does it just seem that way? They can do crazy things with time, you know. Stop it, practically. What if it's only been five *hours*? What if they haven't even noticed I'm gone? I'm not supposed to tell what happened here. They say you wouldn't understand. But it's not right to do these things to people! Without permission, and without explaining anything! It's inhuman. Of course they aren't human, that's the thing. They can disguise themselves. As anything. John Carpenter got that part right. That was a good film, but it was too negative. *The Thing*, starring Mr. Kurt Russell. And Kurt had to be a macho guy, naturally, and so naturally all the creatures are bad. Which is not right. Some of them are good, I can tell you. In fact, I would say that most of them are good. Not the big white guy in the clear glasses who works nights. Not Roper. And there are other bad ones, but most of them are good.

I've seen things you wouldn't believe. That's why we aren't supposed to tell you. Because you wouldn't believe it. It's not the time for you to begin believing. I don't know why they picked me. I guess they think it's time for me. Their ships are sometimes disguised as helicopters. You can tell by the light. It is the brightest light you've ever seen. You can't look into it without it hurting. I don't think they *want* to hurt us. They forced me to lie down. In a cubicle. It was cool and damp and it smelled bad. They put the bright light on me and looked me over. All over. They seemed quite concerned, about my burns from the truck. They checked me all over to see if I was hurt. Because I *was* hurt. It was like I was paralyzed. There was never just one of them. They were always with another one, or in a group. They *looked* human, most of them. Humanoid, I guess is what they are. They just touch you with their hand or an instrument and you go numb. At first it hurts a lot, for an instant, but then it doesn't hurt at all. You can't feel anything, and you can't move. You just lie there. You can't believe that you are just lying there, not saying anything, not protesting, but you can't. You just can't. Sometimes there are computers there and the beings are putting data into the computers while they do these things to you. And they are always taking pictures. There are balconies, and sometimes there are other beings watching from above. There isn't much furniture. You can't always tell by looking at them whether they are male or female, but somehow, you just...know. The shorter ones are the helpers. The taller ones are in charge. That is definite. The small ones especially stare at you. It is dangerous to look at them. Somehow you know that, so you try not to look in their eyes. Listen, I'm worried about Ameen. Saddam put his brother in here and he never came out. He did something, I don't know what, and one night the Mukhabarat came and got him and brought him here and he was never seen again. That's why Ameen hates Saddam so much. And he said if he ever was put in here he would kill himself. Somebody here *did* kill himself. Maybe you can find out if Ameen is here. There must be a list. Maybe he escaped.

[*He picks up the baseball, throws it to the floor so that it bounces up and back into his hand.*]

Like Mr....

[*He throws the ball against the floor again.*]

Steve…

[*He throws the ball against the floor again, smiles.*]

McQueen. *The Cooler King*. Yeah, man. Go to Rashid Street, to my shop. Ameen might be there, keeping an eye on things for me. He is my best friend.

[*He sets the baseball on the bunk bed.*]

I can't talk about the situation here. I am personally of the opinion that they want to take over. I think where they come from is… running out of energy, whatever sustains them, and they have to leave that place. And so they need to take over here. This is the preparation. They are exploring, to see if this is a good place for them to come and live. They show us pictures, wide-screen, 360 degrees. In 3-D, no special glasses required. Pictures of things we see all the time, but stopped noticing. The gutters running like sewers; the marshlands disappeared; the pipelines burning in Kuwait; the sky black with smoke. We tried to tell them that it isn't all our fault. That Saddam did a lot of this shit. That the sanctions did a lot of it. Then the Americans, and in reaction to the Americans, the fucking Fedayeen. But they didn't want to hear any excuses. They know the Garden of Eden, the original *Jannat Adn* was *just a few miles from here!* From where we are standing, did you know that? Oh, yes, they know what they are doing by coming here. And they want us to realize what we are doing to the earth. If they are going to come here and take over, well, there has to be something left, after all. Something they can use. To sustain their race. Enable them to go on, to continue.

When they make us strip, I think it has something to do with reproduction. So they come here in disguise, and their ships are disguised. And they make us strip and they do these experiments so they can learn about us. I think that when they make us lie down naked on top of one another it is all a misunderstanding. And when they make us touch ourselves... masturbate...it is only to find out how the penis works, something like that.

[He struggles with what he is feeling.]

I do not think I can go back to the life I had before. I don't want to go back. I think I will never see my wife again. I don't think I could be with her anymore. Not now. And Layla will be fine in the care of her mother, who was always much more strict with her than I was. I spoil her, I admit it. I don't have much time left, but I will tell you what I think. I think that these beings may be...angels. I think they are beings between us and God. It is not always easy to recognize them. In John Carpenter's film, for example, when Norris has a heart attack and they get him up on the gurney and the doctor climbs up with the defibrillator to try to shock him back to life and Norris's chest suddenly *opens up*, then *closes quick* on the doctor's arms, cutting them off at the elbows, then *opens up again* and another head, smaller, uglier, with sharper teeth but recognizably Norris, rises up out of his chest on a writhing neck, well, it is horrible, no question.

And of course Kurt Russell immediately turns his flamethrower on it and kills it. But who is to say that the monster was not really an angel. In disguise. Or just angry. We will never know, because Kurt Russell killed it. Maybe he just didn't recognize it for what it was. Or maybe he did. I don't know. Would that we knew what the nightly visitant is. Last night the visitant was E.T. Right here in my cell. I knew there was going to be another examination when they brought out the sheets and blankets and hung them over the bars so that no one could see in. I appreciate that. Privacy is good. They made me strip, which I hate to do, but I have gotten somewhat used to it. They needed to take another sample of some kind, I suppose. They never say. Four of them held me down, facedown on the bunk here. Then E.T. was there. I recognized him, even though he was wearing fatigues like the others. He is short and ugly and his head is too big for his body and his eyes are huge. He looked at me. I tried not to look at him. He held up his finger and waved it back and forth in front of my face until I looked up. He was smiling, and his finger was glowing because he was E.T. Then he put the glowing finger up my ass.

[*He struggles with what he is feeling.*]

It hurt and I cried out for God's help. He put it in my ass, the others were all laughing, and then he took it out again.

[*He looks at the floor for a moment, then looks back up at us.*]

I believe I am leaving here tonight. They have examined me. All tests have been done, and the results are in. I've been inoculated against smallpox and diphtheria. There is no history of liver disease in my family. I have assured them of my complete cooperation. Tonight the impossible light will come down at the proper angle to form a ramp of energy from here to there. A guide will float us up the ramp straight...through...the bars. *AMEEN!...YOUR FRIEND IS NOT MAD!* Straight through the bars to the ship, which is waiting for us. It will be...as if...I am a full bucket, pulled up from the well's darkness, then lifted out and up into the light. *AMEEN!...GOD HAS GIVEN HIS ANGELS CHARGE OVER US!* We live in the night ocean, wondering, "What are these lights?" The ship...The ship is a wheel of light, turning in the firmament.

[*A very bright light comes on above the cell, shines down through a grill in the ceiling.*]

A secret, turning in us, makes the universe turn.

[*The light is moved back and forth by someone above the cell.*]

I have my jumpsuit. I am ready. I'm ready to go into the ship. I'm ready to go.

[*We hear the sound of heavy boots on the metal grill. Lights fade, leaving just the overhead light shining down on the man in the orange jumpsuit.*]

[*Blackout.*]

Rick Pulos

Decades Apart: Reflections of Three Gay Men

from

The Best American Short Plays 2008–2009

Author's Note:

These are the stories of men past and present that were shaped and sculpted from love, fear, death, pain, pleasure, happiness, loneliness, addiction, and illness. Their stories are your stories. Your kids' stories. Your grandkids' stories. They are your brothers. They are God's children. They are individuals. They are Americans. They are beautiful. They are you. They are gay.

BOB
(1979, San Francisco)

[*Media: Image that recalls 1970s San Francisco, with music that clearly defines the disco mood of the time and place. BOB sits in a yoga position and breathes heavily.*]

I never knew Harvey.

[*Media: Harvey Milk.*]

I only knew of him. I mean, it was news

[*Media: News report of Mayor Moscone and Harvey Milk's assassination.*]

and I slightly paid attention. I know I walked down Castro Street one day and wandered into that camera shop and bought something. Something. I met him in person. I'm sure I flirted with him. But I didn't vote for him. I didn't vote for anyone. I did walk with the others in the vigil, though.

[*Media: Candlelight vigil.*]

I was so stoned, though. And there were so many hot men. Who could tell who was straight or gay? Nobody seemed to care. You can be a drag queen and nobody cares. All kinds of people will come to see you. You can have an Afro—even if it's gone out of style and nobody cares. These are good times, even in the face of tragedy. Everyone seems to be on our side.

Finally, oh man, it's so good to be in touch with yourself and the city you love. I feel so much love. Jesus, I've had more sex in the '70s than most people have in their lifetimes. And all of it felt good.

[*Media: Images of Castro Street.*]

I never felt bad or guilty or dirty or sad or lonely. I feel fine. I feel love everywhere. For the first time in my life, I really feel good.

PATRICK
(1985, New York City)

[*Media: Imagery that recalls 1980s New York City, with music that defines the coke sniffing, AIDS fearing, greediness of the time and place. Useful images might include Nancy Reagan, subway trains overrun with graffiti, and executives in suits crowding NYC streets.*]

I voted for Reagan. Twice!

[*Media: Ronald Regan with an American flag proudly in the background.*]

I'm not ashamed to say it. Why should I be? It feels like every single fag in New York City hates me for my political views, but they have no problem fucking each other to death. I'm protecting myself and this body. This is all I have. It's gotten to a point where all I see are sick faces.

Even the healthy ones look like death to me. Too much decadence and overindulgence has run amuck in the city. I used to see sexy bodies and transcending smiles, but now the bodies seem emaciated and teeth are falling to the floor everywhere.

[*Media: Rock Hudson turning from gorgeous to a skeleton.*]

Well, I'm not bending down to pick those teeth up. I'm not getting my hands dirty for people that take unforgivable risks. I'm not waking up one morning and looking in the mirror to see the back of my mouth when I smile—it's not happening to me! I spend a lot of nights at home.

[*Media: a map of America engulfed in flames.*]

I spend a lot of days at funerals. Men I loved and men I've made love to. So I can't put myself out there and maybe that's made me cold and maybe that's made me smart. Maybe being cold and smart is the only defense against all this suffering.

DANNY
(1990s, Los Angeles)

[*Media: Imagery that recalls 1990s Los Angeles, with music that defines the crystal meth club kid craze that swept the gay scene (then and now). Useful images might include Bill Clinton and Monica*]

Lewinsky, fabulously decadent outfits, and anything with Matthew Shepard.]

I take this pill and everything is fine. Just fine.

[*Media: Pills tumbling out of bottles.*]

I am invincible. I will live forever. I take them down with a cocktail in hand.

[*He swallows.*]

Just like that! And I am ready to go all night up and down Santa Monica Boulevard. I walk into the club with my entourage in tow and all eyes fall on me. I glimmer in the club lights. My face is alive. I know my life is fierce. No one doubts that. And I have no fear. No inhibitions. No limitations. People might think I live recklessly, but I don't care. I'm like a 1990s James Dean.

[*Media: James Dean.*]

I'm a fucking rock star! I'm out living and breathing. One day, I might be too skinny to walk or dance and even too out of it to talk, but no matter what happens to me, I'm having my fun now, tonight. I'm no scarecrow in a field with blood running down my face.

[*Media: Matthew Shepard.*]

I'm not letting anyone fuck with me. You might not like the way I live, but you're gonna let me live. Because I'm not ready to die. I'd rather see you rot in hell before I let you get your hands on me and take any of this away. So back the hell up, step aside and let me move forward.

PATRICK
(1980s, a Record Store,
New York City)

[Media: Images of a distorted yet bustling and hurried NYC. Images might include packed sidewalks or NYC transportation hubs or piles of trash on street corners in the city.]

I see so much greed and so much gluttony. I see people with a hand out while they hold a crack pipe in the other. I've become totally immune. Most of the time these dumb-ass Democrats are standing up at the podium, their pants wide open while some hooker blows them underneath, and preaches how you and I need to fix all this. We must help those who can't help themselves. I'm tired of hearing about it all. How about I help myself and the ones I love? How about that? All of a sudden in this great city, in this grand country, the glue is a mix of dirty money, cocaine, and Aqua Net. What happened here? Walking down these vast city streets, I see the heat burning through Hefty bags left out on the curb too long. I smell the stench of all these filthy bastards.

They're taking their time, digging their heels in and fortifying trenches, and they are slowly tearing the heart and soul of this great nation to bits. One fix at a time. The more I think about it, the more I feel sick inside. Just to get away from it all, I walk into my favorite record store, a small dopey place I'd been going to for years in the West Village. A hole in the wall with a decent selection. You know the kind, where people let you do your thing and don't mess with you. Nobody raises an eyebrow if you ask about some offbeat composer no one has ever heard. I go all the way in the back of the store, past the rock, the gospel, the country section, right into the classical music—an oasis, of course stuck right next to the very gay Broadway show section. Why these record stores have this kind of odd organization, I could never understand. It's like putting filet mignon next to beef jerky. Anyways, I'm minding my own business, flipping through the newest editions, when he turns to me and says: "You hear anything about this new show on the West End, *Phantom of the Opera?*" And I say, very shortly, "No," without even taking one glance. I simply continue flipping through the records at a much more fierce pace. Why is this guy bothering me anyways? But he doesn't stop. He's persistent. "I've heard it is absolutely amazing. I mean, Webber's done some amazing work and they're all saying this beats anything he's ever done. That certainly says something." And then I make my first mistake—I look at him. I barely manage to say, with such despise and attitude, "Sorry, I don't follow musicals." And he smiles. You ever choke on a smile? He's perfect. He's gorgeous. His eyes, even his teeth. Why is he even talking to me? And then it happened. It's so depressing when you give into your heart. The only power you have over anything else is your self-control. But infatuation is the most incurable infection. And once it has a grip, you don't. I could rub myself this way or that way, I could start a fire in my imagination that would satisfy my every sexual whim. But a single stroke, a delicate touch, a foul-mouthed breath, anywhere on my skin by him and I was like an AIDS article, stuck ten pages deep in a newspaper, so far away from the front page of myself that I was unrecognizable to myself. I turned my back on so many things so many times that when this sweet creature came along, I was lost. Hopelessly lost. I felt protected by him. I was safe. I was comfortable. Suddenly, I wasn't angry anymore. Most of you have been there and some of you have been back again. This was not like some crazy trumped-up crush. This was it. It. Relationships are exactly like a Rubik's Cube.

[*Media: The Rubik's Cube.*]

There are many faces, many colors, everything gets mixed up, and one wrong move can send you further and further away from the goal. Which is, as far as I can tell, growing old together while facing the decades in our past. That's all I could think about. Imagine the poppy field in *The Wizard of Oz*. He's my poppy field. That stench, that contempt I had been seeing all around this city, my clenched fists, gone. Blood returned to my knuckles for the first time in years, my hair felt like it was growing again and not falling out strand by strand. I was afraid, for the first time in my life, I was afraid. I was afraid because I felt responsible for someone other than myself.

DANNY
(1999, West Hollywood
and Beverly Hills)

[*Media: Any image or lighting that allows* DANNY *to be beautiful in the club fights. Also, any imagery that might recall the advent of the Internet.* DANNY *dances almost as if he were a go-go boy, then the lights come up as if the club night has ended.*]

So, I'll admit this, only to you.

[*Whispering.*]

This life is not so fabulous. Don't let anyone else know; I'll fuck you all up if you do. Some of us need to do things that others would find appalling. I find them amusing. Yes, amusing. Maybe I've always hustled in one way or another. But all these other more descriptive terms with dirty underlying meanings suddenly popped into my mind, like escort, male prostitute, and whore. Don't get me wrong, I asked to be called a whore many times, with many men, in many beds. But knowing that money would change hands made it feel so dirty and so sexually exciting. Which was the absolute last thing I ever thought would get me going on this planet. Okay. So the Internet was like this web of communication. Ultra-technology or some bullshit like that, so they say. Send. Receive. Send, receive. Little balls of energy squirting across the planet in the blink of an eye. All types of people entangled in a web of fascination and flirting with their darker anonymous sides. Me? I used it. For my benefit. Maybe you did too. And maybe, it used me. It's so hard to tell. But goddamn it, it got me through some of the hardest weeks. So I found my "John" on gay.com, aka the men's network, or as I call it, the men's warehouse, suits optional. On gay.com I could say what I wanted, how I wanted, and act as dumb as a hooker or dealer at the hottest street corner in town. And nobody was paying attention. His "profile"—Ed, that's the name he gave me— seemed fine. Not f-i-n-e fine but just fine. I negotiated for about five minutes. Yep, that's all it took. I had what he wanted and he had what I needed. I immediately hopped into my super-compact Geo Metro convertible, top down, and pushed my right foot down so hard on that damn accelerator that it was like I was instantly in overdrive. The smog-infused Los Angeles air whipped by me whistling "Dixie."

[Media: Los Angeles traffic.]

Now, any right-minded person would have asked me right then: What is going through your fucking mind? Rent, bills, cigarettes, booze, drugs. No. Wrong. I was hungry;

desperately hungry after a long night of dancing and partying. I wanted a fucking Grand Slam Breakfast from Denny's.

[*Media: A Denny's sign rises into clouds like a soul to heaven.*]

Warm fucking eggs, some goddamn flapjacks, and some seriously processed sausage links. I didn't care that the maple syrup would be fake. In my mind, all I could hear was: Sausages. Pancakes, mmmmm. Warm eggs.

[*Media: Sausages, pancakes, and eggs in various states and, if possible, with the human body.*]

Maybe that was in my stomach. Whatever. So, yes, I was driving like a motherfucker. I mean, like a bat outta hell, and all these assholes were flipping me off, calling me names (even worse than a fucking whore), and I just turned the radio up louder and louder and louder to drown out all those dumb asses. I was weaving down Wiltshire Boulevard. In and out. In and out. In and out. I was in high pursuit of a Grand Slam Breakfast. And nothing was stopping me. Sausages. Pancakes, mmmmmm. Warm eggs.

[*Media: Sausages, pancakes, and eggs in various states and if possible with the human body.*]

Now, I was approaching Beverly Hills, where this guy's place of business as located. Where we planned our little rendezvous. This was not some silly 90210 surprise for me—

the more high class, the more ass they like. I passed by security like smog through a crack. And for a second I thought, he's looking funny at me. That dumb ass in the rent-a-cop outfit is looking at me funny. And immediately my arrogance was like some sort of streak of anger that flashed through me instantly, and I darted him a look that reduced him to some kind of ant, a peon, a cockroach. Yep, in the wake of me becoming some kind of prostitute for processed pork, I had some balls to judge someone else making an honest living. Who the fuck was I?

[*Beat.*]

I was the hottest motherfucker to ever grace that Bev Hills office build! I walked in as if I were headed for an interview to take over the CEO position at Coca-Cola or GE. I was all attitude. Sausages. Pancakes, mmmmm. Warm eggs.

[*Media: Sausages, pancakes, and eggs in various states and if possible with the human body.*]

And then...I met Ed. Fat ass, not so bad in the face, slightly balding...Ed. What a dumb motherfucker. He bullshit-talked me about his PR job and his asshole co-workers, pointing things out on the way to his private office like the lovely plants at the receptionist's desk and the very expensive furniture in the high-tech conference room. Was this guy for real? Sausages. Pancakes, mmmmm. Warm eggs.

[Media: Sausages, pancakes, and eggs in various states and, if possible, with the human body.]

Finally, we were in his private zone. And as soon as he closed that door and he rubbed his wedding ring apprehensively, I got so fucking horny, I thought I'd blow a load right there. I don't know why. But I held it all together for the money shot. You know what I mean? The concept of a condom never came up in our chat on gay.com. I don't even know if that conversation happened for most of us who were bouncing around that website. We all seemed so fearless with the new technology. Fearless and fabulous. Sausages. Pancakes, mmmmm. Warm eggs.

[Media: Sausages, pancakes, and eggs in various states and, if possible, with the human body.]

I was so horny at this point. Hungry and horny. Not the best combo, in my opinion. So while I was pulling down my pants and bending over his neatly organized desk—a desk littered with paperweights, probably gifts from his wife or kids, from various tropical and cultural destinations—I just begged for it. I couldn't help it. And that got him going like some animal in the wild. And I gritted my teeth: Sausages. Pancakes, mmmnnn. Warm eggs.

[Media: Sausages, pancakes, and eggs in various states and, if possible, with the human body.]

And I swear to God I saw a memo on his desk from some fuck-face executive at Denny's. Maybe it was IHOP or the Waffle House—it was there, IT WAS THERE! I swear. Sausages. Pancakes, mmmmmm. Warm eggs.

[*Media: Sausages, pancakes, and eggs in various states and, if possible, with the human body.*]

[*Breathing heavily.*]

And it was over like that. Like a gay.com chat gone wrong, where the guy just shuts down all his windows and disappears and never chats you up again. He started counting under his heavy breathing. Twenty, forty, sixty, eighty. He was counting so fast that I could barely hear myself thinking: Sausages. Pancakes, mmmmm. Warm eggs.

[*Media: Money.*]

BOB
(1970s, a Bathhouse
in San Francisco)

[*Media: Disco music mashed up with images of men at bathhouses.*]

[BOB *has a simple white towel wrapped around his waist. He is bouncing around a seedy bathhouse or, for those of you who do not see seediness, a funhouse for gays.*]

Love is like God. You know what I mean. You've heard this before: I can't see God but I knew he exists. Or what about that one when some try to explain all this mystery to you: you can't see the wind but you know it's there because you can feel it. Personally, I think God is a menopausal whacked-out woman. You know the type, comes after you with a quick wit and sharp tongue. Slices you to pieces by seeing right through you. Points out all your faults and highlights all the things you desperately try to hide from the light. Thunder's like that heat that won't stop. Floods are like the floods that won't stop. And men are always doing stupid things that annoy you. That's who God is. This is her wrath. Now I'm not trying to make enemies of any of you religious folk. Far from it. You see, I pray. Hell, I've been to Vegas and I've prayed for the big one. I've been to all the bathhouses, and I prayed for the big one. And I've been to the confessional, and I prayed that the priest would take me in his arms and love me like he loves his God. But what I realized is all that praying is like scratching that space between your neck and your ass crack; it's like you're constantly reaching for something, something. But you can't quite ever satisfy that itch.

We've all been there. The first time I heard "I love you" was the first time a boy unzipped his pants while I was kneeling on the ground.

[*He kneels down.*]

Dear God, Please tell me this will last forever. This feeling.
This love, it makes me feel so special.

Wanted. Unique. Alive. Don't take this from me.

[*He stands.*]

Love is also punishment. At least, that's what I found out that
day. I remember my mother slapping my face: "You don't do
that. That's disgusting." What did I do? I prayed! I was praying.

When you get this. All this foolishness we call life. When
someone like you or me understands this much. Too much...
We should be dead. But that bitch, that beautiful bitch, God,
she wants us to suffer on and on. And we linger in this world,
looking right through it as if through a crystal ball. Maybe
she wants us to see more to learn more, I'm not sure. But I'm
not afraid.

Hell. I walk the halls of the bathhouse cruising for love in
every backroom dark and dank. The odor is delicious:
unwashed socks, boxers stuffed in little lockers—lockers never
cleaned, at least, that's what I imagine. There's this guy or
that guy or, damn it, any guy. Here's the one reason I love
God more than anything: she knows how to have a good
laugh. She can make a man...and she can make a woman...
and she can make a man that acts like a woman and vice versa.
This is some serious comedy.

Think about it. But like a sundae, she tops it off with a
bright delicious cherry, neither you nor me could ever have
dreamed of: fetishes. I don't know why people are so

embarrassed by them. We all have them. Look, you can act like you don't but I know you do.

[*Pointing to audience members.*]

That one likes his nipples gently touched, oh, and she's a real beggar for her hair being pulled, you know, just so...oh, and most of us love dirty filthy sex talk. It's true. And you know what you like. So I never blink when this one or that one asks for whatever's gonna get him going. I mean, all of us have our limits, but sometimes you stretch because it's the only thing you can do when he's all you have going at four in the morning. So out of the blue—and I mean this one was a bit out there—this guy asks me, "Got a Kleenex?" This guy wanted me to sneeze. Sneeze on him?

I've heard it all now! People always get so stressed when you're learning the behavior of new people, but I truly think even the weirdest shit is fascinating. I mean, everywhere I go, from the Castro to the Haight to the Pacific Ocean, even inside the walls of these saunas, I'm like living inside one of those nature film documentaries, you know, on PBS, where they study the lives of lions and tigers in their own natural habitat, in the wild. In my head, I'm always hearing that narrator, "The mating practices of the homosexual are fascinating. Let's watch as the top male approaches the bottom male aggressively, by participating in the tradition of cruising. The top male will look seductively at the bottom male for many moments, often walking by him and then walking by again. There is rarely talking. They will both look for any signs that will initiate the act of coitus." Anyone can choose to look away or run and hide. But that doesn't mean what exists is itself going to evaporate into some mystical wind that no one can truly see: There's always a path and *sometimes* a choice and hope is deceptively wrapped up in the "sometimes" and not even I can believe that it's just confusion or anxiety or injury that makes sense of any path to anything if anything is something anyone would ever want.

DANNY
(1990s, West Hollywood)

[*Media: Religious imagery set against a Los Angeles background.*]

[*He is dressing for a night on the town.*]

You ever see these people out on the street passing out Bibles? What are they trying to do? I mean, I always pass by them as if they are handing out flyers to some seedy straight strip club. Somehow, all the street peddlers seem the same to me, whether they're asking for a dune or trying to hand me a Bible. And it's always all sorts of people doing this. White, black, old, young, ugly, cute. God, the variety of Jesus freaks is frightening! As usual, I'm on my way to a fabulous night out, right. What's left but to have me a good time? When this little punk starts to flirt with me, right. What a great gimmick he had going in West Hollywood. Instead of handing me a Bible, he hands me a card. He says that I can get help. That he used to be like me. That there are others who have broke through the sin. That all I needed was a clear path to God. That it wasn't too late.

Now you gotta understand something: I was curious, no doubt. I mean, a bunch of reformed fags—probably cute and straight-laced, all nice and cleaned up—sitting around in a circle trying to avoid that quick glance at the package or a quick peak at an ass while getting coffee on a break. Of course I just looked him up and down. His smile disgusted me and yet turned me on too. What's up with that? And I said bluntly, "Honey, all paths lead to God. They curve and shift like light refracting. There is no straight path." I bounced away so fast, but he was quick too. As I careened forward towards my perfect night out, I could hear him in the distance reciting the Scripture. And God blessed them, and God said unto them, Be fruitful, and multiply, and replenish the earth: and subdue it: and have dominion over the fish of the sea and over the fowl of the air, and over every living thing that moveth upon the earth.

PATRICK
(Fall 1986, His Apartment,
New York City)

[*Media: Imagery that recalls autumn in New York City.*]

[*He wears a brilliantly white robe.*]

It all gets complicated. That's the way autonomy ends. Or perceived autonomy, if you will. And suddenly you magically realize that there's something more to living than the life you've been leading. And therein lies the problem. Why must I be the one wrapped in a blanket of guilt? Why must I be the one to recognize my limitations just because he loves me so? Why must I see myself when all I want to see is beyond me? Fact. I am not in love nor have I ever been in love. Fact. He turned to me one night with the seriousness of a politician and said bluntly, "I am addicted to you." That's not my problem, I thought. That's not my problem, no way.

[*Beat.*]

I thought. Fact. There is something special about feeling special. My veins worked overtime around him, pumpin' karma through my heart with a vigor unlike any I ever knew. I saw colors in the stars no one should ever see. Red, white, blue. Fact. I was a slave to my own fears. He had a power over me that made me feel desperate for a longer life. A life I spent uncountable hours trying to escape. Fact. I knew I would lose myself to him as soon as he recovered from his addiction. Fact. The people closest to you never recover from the things you wish they could. Fact. He did not die of AIDS or some mysterious pneumonia. Fact. His brain swelled like a balloon and it impaired his vision and his ability to interpret reality. Fact. He died April 5, 1986, under a blanket of mystery.

Actually, under a sheet that depicted the bizarrely happy world of the Smurfs. He loved the Smurfs. He died gasping for more life while I prayed for a swift end. Fact. I looked at the recognizable image of Smurfette on that sheet and slowly began to take my clothes off. Not that I was retreating to some freaky heterosexuality, some oddball fetish that not even my childhood could explain. I wanted so much to just have an ounce of the love he had for me.

[*He takes off his robe and kneels down to touch the body.*]

Fact.

He was still warm. Fact. I felt cold everywhere.

[*He puts his robe back on.*]

What is this thing? What is this disappointment? Is this what everyone should expect from living? From the first breath to the last. Is this what we have to look forward to? They took him away on a dirty, used stretcher. I swear it was still warm from the last one they carted out, from wherever, to wherever. It looked like it was stained with sweat or feces, I don't know what. I couldn't even think about who or what was there before. He was out of my house and out of my life as fast as he came in. And nothing about it was delicate or beautiful or smart. It was...indescribable.

[*Media: Thunder, lightning, and then silence.*]

I didn't even send flowers. I DIDN'T SEND A GODDAMN
SINGLE FLOWER! There was no one to send a simple
condolence to. There was nothing to say, to anyone. So I said
nothing. NOTHING! How can a man feel this much and say
absolutely nothing? His mother claimed the body. She had
already told me I was "uninvited." My friends, oh, the poor
bastards, called on me to say this and that, but most of them
were so tired of death, it was like they were reading from
index cards. It wasn't their fault. And I thought about that
word a lot. Fault. You know, like a lawyer. I thought about
that word, about that language, that term. And I thought...I
thought about a lot of people that I knew and I was hoping to
know better. And I thought about the significance of one
man, one woman, one child. I thought about all those
memories, washed away too soon. Lost. And I thought about
God. Because God was the only man I ever knew that ever
knew me. And he knew me in my faults and my follies.
Whatever any of that meant. And of course I tried to feel so
much for those who had suffered and those who were
suffering but I was so chained to my misery that I could
hardly care. I'm not a crier. My mother taught me to never
ever let anyone see me cry. So I never cry. Even before God.
But she never told me not to think. To think about why, why
any of this is the way it is. In the dark. In the corners of our
houses, our apartments, our minds, whatever you feel
comfortable calling it, in those spaces, you and me see
ourselves and we know who we are. We have dreams beyond

those walls, but prisoners have dreams beyond theirs. And so? And so, the chore, I feel, that you and I have, as residents of these spaces, is simple: Figure out more. Figure out more about yourself.

When he left my house. He left a scent. But more importantly. He left a thought. And as I go through the daily grind, brushing away the filth from my teeth, looking in that mirror, I can't help but ask myself, I can't help but taking a silly little pulse to find some kind of vital sign, in all this, in all that has happened to me, in all that has happened to my friends, in all that has ever happened, I must ask: Who am I? Who am I?

BOB
(New Year's Eve, 1979,
Castro District, San Francisco)

[*Media: The ball dropping, showing the start of the 1980s, punctuated by wild fireworks that recall the birth of a new decade.*]

Anyone could have guessed disco would die. Please, that was a given. I mean, we all hoped Anita Bryant would, but that was just wishful thinking. And we all loved screwdrivers too much to stay off that juice for too long. I mean, I guess we made our statement but who did it really change? There was this euphoria out on the Castro in December 1979. There was this I can do what I want attitude. It was sexy and empowering. Guys were sleazy and it was cute. Girls were out mouthing off against the men and that was totally necessary. There was a sense of community and communication. Sure some guys and gals were still hidden from view, but people kept getting braver and braver by the minute. Time and virtue seemed to be on our side. And it felt like a lot of people were coming around to support us. So as the ball dropped in New York City and the balls came out on the Castro, the 1980s looked to be one of the best decades for my sisters and brothers. I could feel it all over, everywhere. Things can only get better from here.

DANNY
(Fall 1999, Los Angeles)

[*Media: A vicious gay bashing mixed in with images of* DANNY *bruised and beaten. Any news media that reports a hate crime.*]

[DANNY *speaks over the media offstage.*]

The things I've done to my body. The constant abuse that I mistook for pleasure. Sometimes if you're one of the lucky ones, there appears a moment of clarity, or oxygen magically materializes while you're drowning in a sea of murkiness in a horrid, real-feeling dream. My oxygen, my clarity, surfaced as a fractured cheek bone, several cracked ribs, a displaced shoulder, scrapes, bruises, even partial loss of vision in one eye.

[He enters, moving slowly, using a cane.]

I'll never dance the same. But that is very insignificant.
What happened to me could happen to any of you. I was
truly minding my own business. I remember leaving the club.
I had had some drinks but nothing to write home about. I
never saw any of them coming. I lied in the hospital bed, I
could barely see through all the bandages, and I tried to piece
it all together. Cops, nurses, doctors, all swarmed around me
like flies to shit. A few people, I'd only call acquaintances,
now came in quick, going through the motions, and looked
down at me like I was some kind of freak. I didn't want
visitors, I didn't want that pity, I never wanted to see that
face—that telling face—by some people who in that fucked-
up way were trying to tell me somehow that all of this was my
fault. That I'd asked for it and that they had always warned
me I was heading for trouble. I could barely mumble, my lips
were so swollen. So I pretended I couldn't talk at all. It was
better that way. I had all these feelings suddenly. They
weren't exactly feelings. It was actually one immense crude
sensation: rage. And I thought: I want a gun. I need a fucking
gun. I want to shoot every motherfucker that fucks with me.
I mean, this is what I'm thinking in that hospital bed. I want
to wipe out all the idiots in the world. You know the type,
department store clerks that act like you're going to steal
something, losers that can't get an order right at McDonald's,
DMV clerks looking up goddamn who knows what on their

little computer screens with such contempt and mightiness. Am I really just a number? Reduced to this old address or that old car?

It's amazing when you become a headline. All of a sudden, you realize you're not a number. What happened to me wasn't front-page news, but it was bigger than three lines in the police blotter. "GAY MAN BEATEN BY TWO TEENAGERS" "TEENS GONE WILD ON HOMOSEXUAL IN WEST HOLLYWOOD" I never remembered these guys' faces. I remember the soles of their boots. I remember numbness in my head. I remember the taste of blood and concrete. I remember wanting to laugh at it all. Even while it was happening.

When I went to court and looked at them, I felt a new sensation. A difficult feeling. More complex than love or hate or disgust or respect. I felt compassion. It did not help that they were kind of attractive all dressed up in suits and ties, I'm not going to lie about that....

But I felt deeply: they were wrong and they should be punished, but something seems off in all this. Don't I have a responsibility to try to understand whatever it is that set them into motion? Don't I have a responsibility as a human being to be compassionate and learn from everything that led these boys to that moment? Was it their parents, their culture, their rage, our country's temperament, their testosterone...what the fuck was it?! And suddenly, I cried on the stand like some goddamn sissy-boy. Jesus, that really did them in for the trial and the sentencing. That was not my intention. What I found out was that I had a job. That I was needed for something other than to be the life of the party. That I had responsibilities.

And maybe, just maybe, I could raise a mirror to some other kid somewhere else and stop this from happening to someone else.... I'm not excusing this. Any of this hatred. I just want to learn more. But. And I say this without hesitation. Maybe our differences, our fears, these things we all pile up behind our eyes, are just little nuggets of light waiting to be seen. If there's a chance we could see them before they turn into fists full of fears, each and everyone one of us should take that chance, open that door, and walk through it with a single intention: to better understand each other. And the only way any of us can be understood is for each of us, in our own way, to stand up and be seen even in all our ugliness because there is beauty in ugliness. Drag it all out into the streets, shine a light right on each and every face here and out there and take a moment to see what's really going on. This next millennium, this new millennium, we must all stand in the light and be seen.

[*Media: Useful media here would be a current hot issue from LGBT community regarding human rights issues, whether from America or abroad.*]

[*Performed either live or through media.*]

I am not a single reflection.
I am light refracting. I am many parts.
I am not the sum.
I am moving through life.
Life is moving through me.
I am who I am in a single moment.
I will never be perfect.
And I wouldn't want to be.

[*Media: This has happened. This is happening now.*]

Part II

Monologues for Women

Adam Kraar

excerpt from

Hearts and Minds

from

The Best American
Short Plays 2006–2007

REBECCA   Okay, class. Listen up. We need to focus. I want you all to close your eyes. Just do it. Now take a series of deep, deep breaths.

[*As if getting him into line.*]

…Rudi. Take the breath all the way down and slowly let it out.…Keep breathing.…Somewhere inside your body is a tight ball. I've got one right now in my stomach. I want you to send the breath to wherever that tight ball is, let the breath dissolve that hard little ball…and then breathe out the molecules that came off of the ball.…Do it again. Rudi, I want you to really see the ball.…All right, Rudi, then see the bialy. Just keep breathing…

[RUDI *appears in the doorway, upstage. He apparently overheard her talking to herself, and now leans in to see what's going on.* REBECCA *does not see him.*]

...Now the ball—or the bialy—has disappeared, and the only thing is your breath, coming in, slowly, and going out, slowly...and the molecules of your breath are swirling around this classroom, mixing together with the molecules of other students and teachers, who teach and learn, and pour out ideas and passions. Imagine if you will molecules of people who lived and died, and spoke and wrote long before us—those particles are here too. The molecules are all mixing together, connecting in new ways, actually creating something unprecedented. With each breath, what you're breathing in is different than what you just breathed out. And that altered air is filtering into your bloodstream, going into your brain, pumping into your heart....Take a moment and listen to the new air, surging through you. It's not just your breath or my breath. It's the oxygen we all have to share in order to survive. And if we really let it in, it can change everything....Now, open your eyes. And please turn your chairs so you can face each other.

Bruce Levy

excerpt from

Sada

from

The Best American
Short Plays 2002-2003

SADA Ahhh, yes. Miss Sada Cohen soon to be Mrs. Sada
Jacobson was real, as you say, "hot." And this one [*Referring to
another picture.*] was taken at the beach at Coney Island just
before we were married. Jake was handsome and strong.
From a good family but he knew his way around. From the
Bronx. A little rough around the edges...like you. Me? I was
a princess from Brooklyn. We met through friends. He was
my hero. This day Jake was taking me home from the beach
on the subway train. Such a nice day, such fun, we swam, we
ate ice cream and hot dogs, we played skeet ball on the
boardwalk, you know skeet ball? [...] You have a ball you
throw up a ramp and try to get it into the holes with the most
points. Then you take your points and trade them for a prize.
[...] Well, on this day Jake played and played and played until
he was able to get me a big pink stuffed bear. It cost him more

than if he would have bought me a bear but he wanted me to have that bear so bad to take home with me. So we get on the subway train and Jake had his arm around me and I was hugging the pink bear when hooligans came onto the train to rob us. They stood at each door of the train and one ruffian went to each person and pushed and shoved and took their jewelry and money. Jake and I were sitting in the corner. Jake drew me closer to him and whispered in my ear. Don't worry, kiss me and make believe we don't notice. Oy, in public we kissed and hugged and I shook and trembled and squeezed the big pink bear tight. The man guarding the door near us had a stump for one of his arms. He was wearing a T-shirt and you could see. At the next stop people tried to run off the train but the men at the doors pushed them back. [...] Yes! And Jake stood up and gently took the man's stump in his hand and said, with such a heavy Brooklyn accent from where I don't know, "Hey, have fun but done hurt nobody too much okay, my friend?" The guy said, "Nahhh, done worry, done tell no one, k?" Jake said, "Who'm I gonna tell"? We got off the train and Jake told the token man and the token man called the police, who boarded the train at the next stop and arrested them. My hero, Jake.

[*Smelling onions.*]

Oy, oy! The onions.

[*To stove.*]

I always tell Rebecca, don't burn the onions! The egg pancake is never good when you burn the onions. Gentle. It has to be gentle. So...I burn the onions! I yell at my daughter-in-law, "It's not good if you burn the onions!"

Dano Madden

excerpts from

Beautiful
American Soldier

from

The Best American
Short Plays 2005–2006

LAMIYA English. I'm going to learn English. I'm going to go to a university in America. Probably in New York or California. And I'm going to learn beautiful English. Are you listening to me? You've no right to be angry. Do you want to know why I'm going to learn English? Because I'm in love. I am. I'm in love with an American soldier. Don't tell Mama or Papa.

[*Beat.*]

I met him at a checkpoint. The American soldier, the one I'm in love with. There were a lot of soldiers. They were checking us for guns and bombs. I admit, it wasn't love at first sight. At first sight I just wanted my American soldier. His hair was cut so close to his head. His face was freshly shaven. It was a hot day and I could see little beads of sweat on his forehead. He was yelling, motioning for me to come to him. So I walked over to this soldier. He wasn't as large as some of the others—but his muscles were smooth and strong.

[*Beat.*]

Ula? I know you hate this kind of talk. You have to listen, though. You have to listen if you're just going to sit there. We can still make it. You're the one giving up.

[*Beat.*]

I tried to see his eyes, but they were hidden behind his sunglasses. I looked down to the ground and I noticed, beneath all of his weapons and his belts—I noticed him bulging, through his pants. And he started to check me. Feeling me. Up my sides. In between my legs. So gentle. Feeling me all over—searching me, trying to find a weapon or a bomb. I felt his breath on my neck. I imagined the bulge in his pants pressing up against me. I began to wish that I did have explosives strapped on—all over my body. How wonderful if my soldier had discovered a bomb on me. He'd take me away to a tent. And he'd carefully start to take my clothes off until all that was left was the bomb and the tape holding it on—over my naked body. I'm certain that my soldier is very skilled and he would remove the bomb and all of its pieces safely, one by one. He would remove pieces from my arms and my back and my stomach and my chest. Slowly. Until my body was completely bare. The bulge in his pants growing, in spite of his concentration. His mouth so near my neck, my chest. His breathing getting heavier. The bomb completely removed, but his hands continuing to gently search my body. Both of us sweating from the heat of the midday sun—his breath all over my chest, his lips so near my mouth, my back arched and he'd take me. Right there in the dusty tent. Pieces of the bomb all around us.

[*Beat.*]

Ula! You're so boring! Just yell at me if you're angry. We still have time. The reception has only just begun.

[*Beat.*]

The soldier finished checking me and—I love him. Do you want to know why? All you have to do is ask me.

[*Beat.*]

I could leave without you. I'm sure I could find the way. Our sister is married by now, but the best part—the singing, the dancing, the eating. We can still make it.

[*Beat.*]

I can play this game too, you know. I can. And I'll win.

[LAMIYA *sits down dramatically on the opposite side of the tree, demonstrating her ability to "not talk" to her sister. Pause.*]

How about a new game? Yes? Okay. I have a little journal here. Lately I've been writing about the American soldier I'm in love with. Here. Blank pages. Now. You write, on this page, write why you're angry at me. I can't imagine what I've done wrong. Nonetheless, you write. For example: "I am angry because we are late for our sister's wedding and I think it's Lamiya's fault." Or... "I am angry because it turns Lamiya on when soldiers check her for bombs." Or... "I'm angry. Just angry. Because that's my personality."

[*Beat.*]

You can write now. Please.

[*Beat.*]

Come on, Ula! We're wasting time! You used to be my favorite sister. Yesterday I would've said Khaireya was the biggest pain. Always flirting with everyone. Makes me crazy. But *this*, this, whatever *this* is. Moodiness. Stubbornness. Forget it. You are no longer my favorite. You are a pain. Just like Khaireya. Congratulations.

[*Pause.*]

I know why you're angry. You're angry because all of your sisters have a husband. Except me. But—I am the youngest and the prettiest. I have time. As of…oh…about forty-five minutes ago, Shilan is married. And that leaves only the two of us who have no husband. The youngest and the oldest. That's why you refuse to go with me to the reception.

[*Beat.*]

That's stupid, you know. The reason you haven't married yet is because Papa adores you. The way he talks about you, the way he tells his friends how smart you are, how funny. I think, in Papa's eyes, there are no suitable men for you. None worthy.

[*Beat.*]

So don't be angry that Shilan is getting…well…is married by now. We all want to be Papa's favorite. But you are. Only you. Lucky you. Be happy.

[*Beat.*]

Come on. Tell me to shut up. Tell me why it is inappropriate to fall in love with an American soldier. Tell me in great detail why it is my fault we are lost. Or let's talk futbol. Even Mama cannot make you shut up. Speak, speak, speak, speak. Please.

[*Beat.*]

Aren't you hungry at least? Aren't you? I'm starving. Can we at least go for the food? Please? Even if, even if you hate it.

Even if you're angry that nearly all of your sisters are married. We can't miss out on the food. The sweets. The sweets are so succulent at weddings.

[*Beat.*]

So it's official? You're not going to speak to me? Or move from under that tree? Can you signal me in some way?

[*Beat.*]

Alright. I'm going to find my way to the wedding alone.

[*Beat.*]

Okay. Hmmmmm... This road leads in two directions. Hmmm...

[LAMIYA *looks in one direction.*]

West. Hmmm... or is that east? Do you...? Oh, that's right. Forget it.

[LAMIYA *looks in the other direction.*]

There's that way.

[LAMIYA *looks in the other direction.*]

And that way. We came from that way. We've traveled to this point and have not found the wedding. Could you perhaps

point if you feel strongly about a particular direction? What
about that way?

[LAMIYA *points.*]

Or, or ... that way?

[LAMIYA *points the other way.*]

We came from that way. I think.

[*Beat.*]

Fine. I will choose. Good-bye.

[LAMIYA *doesn't move.*]

Aaugh! Ula ! Come on !

[*Singing in the distance. Singing and clanging.* LAMIYA *walks
down the road.*]

Ah-ha! You see that! Look. Coming this way! A man! Perhaps
he'll know the way to the wedding. Maybe he's a guest, one of
Papa's friends.

[*Singing and clanging grows louder.*]

• • • •

ULA   It took such a long time. The soldiers apprehended
several men ahead of us, took them away in jeeps. And ... one

soldier searched my sister, extensively, and she became…
enamored. And…so, so late. I knew we had probably missed
the ceremony. Finally, walking along the road home. Our
papa could never have dreamed we'd be this late. Running. So
late. In the distance they were shooting, firing the
Kalashnikovs into the air—in celebration. Shooting, shooting,
shooting. Running, running, running. Lamiya and I had
missed it. We had missed it. I tried to get my sister to move
faster. Fruit dropping everywhere—I was trying to pick it all
up and—

[*Pause.*]

Suddenly, something knocked us to the ground. A sound.
Deafening. The loudest sound I have ever heard. Planes.
American warplanes. So low, right over our heads, it
seemed. Fruit falling all over, we fell into a ditch. And then
an explosion. So loud. And flames and heat—screaming
planes. Another explosion and another and another and
my sister and I huddled in a ditch. Still another explosion
and on and on and on and on and on. Holding my sister
so tight.

The explosions seemed to go on forever and then—
silence. I opened my eyes. The sky was filled with smoke. The
sun looked pink through the haze. We stayed in the ditch,
afraid to move. So quiet. Now. Birds. The smell of burning. A
cool breeze. And we moved, finally, and saw—

[*Pause.*]

Nothing. Where our house had once stood on the horizon,
we saw nothing.

Nothing, nothing, nothing—walking down the road...we
were lost. And finally, through the smoke, the haze, against
the pink sky, I saw something. Something I recognized. This
tree. I played under this tree growing up, out in the field near
my parents' house. Exactly the same. This tree—this patch of
earth, untouched by anything. But no house. No wedding, no
wedding, no wedding. [...] I always believed we were safe. We
weren't living in Baghdad. My papa thought we were safe.
[...] Now. My entire family. Lamiya and I were supposed to
be there. Everyone was celebrating— [...] My parents, my
sister Khaireya and her husband, Mohammad, my sister
Fatima, her husband, Ahmed, and their son, Raad, my sister
Auood, her husband, Talib, their son, Inad, and their
daughter, Kholood, my uncle Ali, my aunt Hamda, my uncle
Mizhir, my aunt Marifa, my other uncle Ali and his wife,
Somayia, my aunt Fatima, my cousins Siham, Rabha, Zahra,
Hamda, Ali, Hamza, Yasser, Raid, Daham, Wa'ad, Khava, my
uncle Waldemar, my aunt Jasmin, my cousins Mostapha,
Ahmad, and Isra, my sister Shilan, she was the bride, my sister
Shilan and her new husband, Hamid, they were just married
and, of course, all of Hamid's family, everyone I think, my
parents' friends, everyone I think, Shilan, just married, Shilan,
who was probably the second prettiest of my sisters.

Lamiya is of course the prettiest. [...] People came. From the village. And some Americans. We were ghosts, sitting next to this tree. Chaos. People digging and yelling and searching. Focused on everything but us. And then they were gone.

Eileen Fischer

excerpt from

The Perfect Medium

from

The Best American
Short Plays 2007–2008

character

HESTER DOWDEN   a sturdy-looking woman, 55 but looks older, in a high-collared, white-on-white embroidered blouse with a full-length dark green wool skirt. Her black and gray hair is in a bun. She wears reading glasses and takes them on and off and moves them up and down her nose. The glasses are attached to a chain around her neck.

Music for *The Perfect Medium* is composed by Charles Porter, CD Version 7

[*A well-appointed Victorian sitting room in London. Downstage-center, a round table and two chairs. Much moody atmosphere here:*

flickering candles, shadows, dark furniture, a chaise lounge, a piano. Then total blackout. From the blackness, a voice:]

HESTER   Over here.

[*Music: track #1. Pause.*]

Over here.

[*Music: track #1. Pause. Then with annoyance.*]

I said, over here.

[*Lights gradually up on* HESTER. *She is seated at the table covered with a cream-colored lace cloth.*]

Yes. On me. Look at *me.* Let us begin.... Twenty-three years ago Oscar Wilde left the present life and crossed to the other side. It may seem incredible [*To audience.*] to you that he should attempt to send his thoughts back again to a world where his infamy exceeded his good fame and fortune; but here it is, 1923, and Oscar Wilde chooses to send us messages today.

[*Pompously.*]

Are the messages genuine? Does Oscar Wilde still exist?

[*Slight pause.*]

And where exactly is he? ... The public must judge these matters. We will return to them again and again. Yes.... We will. You'll see. Again and again.

[*Pause.*]

Do you understand? Oscar Wilde, the famous Irish writer, the international *bon vivant* and gadfly came to me, Hester Dowden. He spoke to me, here, twenty-three years after his bodily death. Yes ... it is complicated. Yes ... it seems unusual ... yes. But it is true. It happened. Everyone must believe me. Without belief, without faith, what have you?

[*Pause.*]

Those to whom Oscar's words came [*Pats herself proudly.*] can only transmit them to the world.... As for me, I've been a psychic investigator for many years, starting back in Dublin. Now I see clients for private readings here in my London home, and I instruct students in psychic investigations as well. What else can one do? An independent woman must make do. And I do. I do, indeed.... Were you wondering how these messages were received? Let me help. They came through automatic writing and sometimes the messages came through the Ouija board—two well-known methods of psychic communication.

[*She crosses to the piano and plays softly.*]

And as for the automatic writing, one day the messages simply started.

Jill Elaine Hughes

excerpt from

The Devil Is in the Details

from

The Best American Short Plays 2004–2005

You know the really cool thing about all this is, they think I'm dead. And I am, sort of. But not really. Have you ever heard of something called suspended animation, altered physical states? You know, the thing those guys in those old *Alien* movies did to make themselves sleep without aging for years while their ships traveled across the galaxy for decades? Well, that's the closest thing I can think of to explain it. I don't age, you see. Haven't in centuries. They of course think I'm dead, and who could blame them for thinking so? I'm not moving. I have no discernible breath pattern. Not to mention a *very* low body temperature. But I'm not dead. I'm not even unconscious. I feel bad for poor Larry and Sheila here. You have to give them credit for trying. I mean, you at least have

to give Sheila here credit for mixing and distributing all those
lethal gases from stuff she just had sitting around her art
studio when Larry found out the Gangsta Kings wanted poor
old Steve bumped off all nice and quiet-like, with no gunshots
or yucky blood. Actually, quite beautiful work, if I must say so
myself. The perfect crime, you might say. But not *quite*
perfect. There was a little something they overlooked on their
way down here.

Julia Jarcho

excerpts from

The Highwayman

from

The Best American
Short Plays 2005–2006

BESS   Where is this?

[*Pause.*]

The land? The moor. Purple bog. Hi!

[*Beat.*]

Hello. Look out there. I can look out at the land. It'll get darker.

[*Beat.*]

It's nothing for you anyway. I could just make it up and you'd never know the difference. When they say "and it was all a dream," I think, who cares? Tell me a story! I don't care. God. Right there, over there a goat was buried. Many years ago. It

didn't belong to the mother or the father in particular. It was
a family goat. I know goats are popular in jokes, but this isn't
a joke. It's a dream! Ha-ha, who cares, not really. It's a goat.
How do I know? From the inscription. There is a goat
engraved on the tombstone. It doesn't say Beloved Family
Goat, but I know about that for a fact. They loved that goat.
It gave good milk. It ate the garbage. You could pet it at that
time. Now you can only make yourself think so. What it said
was, Here Lies, and then the name of the goat. Who cares? It
wasn't Bess. Or maybe it was. [...] No! Guess what. It wasn't a
goat. Now that I think, it was a donkey. All this time. That
doesn't change much, except the milk and the garbage. But
they adored that donkey. Most donkeys seem to be
unwelcome on this God-given earth, but not that one. Not
this donkey! Why? Because it was so sweet-tempered. You
should see with its kids—all lined up? They were all mules,
but it never complained. The family contemplated having a
portrait done like that, not of themselves. Because you can't
help it if she hands you a mule when the day's come, right?
You really can't. It was a quiet life. I don't want to talk about
the rest. I don't know why I started. Let's just say here lies and
then the name.

• • • •

BESS   After this I have one dream. All right. I think it must
be the darkest time of night. When is that? I think I know.
No, I don't know, that was the dream. And I knew those

things. And I could tell things from the position of planets. Which I recognized. Clouds. I could tell from the clouds what the earth would be? And when they would be on the road? So I would have to go off it. How to find a hedge to go off it into. And know if the hedge is hungry and not go into it then and look again. That this would sometimes be true for miles and I would have to remember that I would have to dig in the ground, because they're on the road now.

I knew how to do that and I had to do that, or also, I wouldn't have to, because there was nothing but me out there, nothing, me moving. Going. Knowing. Looking. Knowing. Not knowing. Knowing again. Or also, a rain like a wind, a moon like a ship, all ocean. I thought, this is what I'm gonna be spraying like all these. Spraying out of here to be then.

• • • •

BESS   Here, in here it's the right heat. I cover the window with earth. People bring in the earth with their shoes. They don't talk to me. It's too dark for them to see me.

[*Beat.*]

Here, in here it's the right heat. I cover the window with fire. The fire lies flat against the pane. It lights up the room and I see my own hands. They don't look old. I know time is over. No one else knows. They can't get it. No one can get in.

[*Beat.*]

Here's the story. There was a girl. She kicked everyone. She said it was so they wouldn't miss her. But it was because they wouldn't miss her. It's a stupid—it's a stupid story. She could never kick anyone. Or do anything or want or think anything.

[*Beat.*]

I know what to tell you. It's only the truth. No questions. Of course this is where I am.

[*Beat.*]

You could come

[*Beat.*]

out.... Why?—I'd like to remind you that the moor is habitable. Habitabitable. Habitabitabitable. Hospitababitle. With life-forms. So savage. Someday something will come in and you'll have to go out there.

[*Beat.*]

So I build up my strength. Emergency measures. I smell my skin. I compare it with my other skill. Things like this'll be helpful. Because I know I've been in here since I was born and no one else. And if someone else was here, he didn't see me. And if he saw me, he's coming back to get me.

[*Beat.*]

Because he would like me.

[*Beat.*]

Would he want me to go, I think he might want me to go with him. I think that's what he would want. There's no way I can do that. Look at me. I've been here my whole life. A quiet life. I used to bring sugar lumps out to the stable. There's a cellar somewhere here, no, a tunnel through, not the cellar, I think there are stairs and there's a, stairs through a room where they keep…beets? Is that possible? Through there, a passage to the stable. I go through there with my hand full of sugar. My hand is dry. Or both. That's how I carry it through the passage, wedged out of the wet land. So I don't set foot out of the inn.

[*Beat.*]

I get there, I get to the stable. There are so many of them. I'm saying this, it's like a pillar of my childhood. I'm not just any one of those little girls. Because these were not a fantasy. They're, they shit and they take a piss, they have spit foaming up, big sour spit, they're covered with scars and their coats, you can't even say coats, they're covered in their skins, is the most you can say. They'll bite, I have the rents some still on me.

[*Beat.*]

I get to the stable, still inside, I have sugar in my hand, that I took from the kitchen. There are so many of them. Everyone put an animal there and went in to drink. When it's the busy season there's fullness of them. And I'm coming down, there's a push-bell the people do when they need something, but then I disappear, I go get the sugar and I go down the stairs into the place and into the place, to see them, to give them the sugar. I don't know how to describe. I said. Filthy. Some are about to die. Some are on their first trip. Whips. They all have four and some have five and some are daughters. Grown-up. I'm here with the sugar. Just here. I put out my hand . . . a tongue comes down, no, teeth. You have to put your hand flat and not get bit. Big teeth. You can tell the work. Eyes like my dumb eyes. You know what they want, it makes them want it more, they want, they would say—they can't, but—no, they wouldn't—it makes them want, they want the saddle blanket and the saddle, the saddlebags and the rein, they want, and the spurs, reins and spurs and hands high, but even done like that they want to go, they want me to take them and go, and they would be better off to go, says their faces, go!

[*Beat.*]

And I say I can't. Just because it's not. What about wind and stripes? But it's not. Anyway he might not come.

• • • •

BESS   What I was feeling. You know metal in your mouth? Sour? It's not you're naked, because he doesn't care about that. He opens your shirt. He doesn't care about that, it's so he can see where to put it. You're, what are you doing, because not that you don't know, you want him to say. He says, Pretty. He takes your eyes. He covers them with his eyes. All you know about is the land around you. Land around you, wet with time. Your bare foot feels the bone coming up under it, up from under the moss, this old bone, smooth as a lip, fills the arc of your foot. He says, Don't move. It's a shoulder bone. He says, Don't you make a sound. Your cheek is wet for me. Listen. You listen. You can hear for miles. Moldering, creeping, growing up against itself, the moor. He says, You're for this. You don't move. The bone under your foot doesn't move. He says, It's inside you already. Inside and outside are the same. He doesn't touch you with his hand. He has no skin. You hear the blood of him. He knows you hear it. Moving, he says. That's what you hear in me. I'm what moves on this land. He says, When I take your last piece of movement you'll understand. Kept. You know that word? And you feel kept on your face, he says, Your face is wet for me. I've made a place for your body. Do you understand? And he kisses you with no mouth but with something cold and sour. Mine.

[*Pause.*]

Do you understand?

Liliana Almendarez

excerpt from

Glass Knives

from

The Best American
Short Plays 2006–2007

JULISSA   It was the first couple of days at school and it was all very new and scary. I meet so many people but not anyone I really want to hang out with. At least not right away. Do you know what I mean? […] Everybody is saying the same thing, hi my name is Jane or John from Hicksville, USA, and I tell them I'm from Brooklyn, New York. They asked me stuff like, "Did you ever see someone get shot? Or mugged? Did you ever have to carry a knife? Were you ever in a gang? Did you go to clubs? Did you hang out in *the Village*?" They acted like it was a whole different country or something. When I told them that I would ride the subway home…they would act weird.

[*Prissy.*]

"Like oh my gawd, I could never live in the city, it's so dangerous." It made me feel like I was an alien. Anyway, one night these people invite me to hang out in Kevin's room to watch *Saturday Night Live*. [...] I thought, what the hell I've got nothing better else to do. So they're all laughing at the stupidest jokes and I sit there thinking it's not that funny. They see that I'm not laughing, so they explain the jokes to me like I'm retarded. I start to get up to leave 'cause I'm just not having any fun. Mark pulls me aside and tells me to ignore them. We start talking and I find out he's from the neighborhood and it's an instant connection. It was so strange...I never thought black guys were cute. You know. [...] Big nose, big lips...lighter is better *para mejorarse la Raza*. That night it was different. Here I am coming from the city, just broke up with Robert, I'm a little too loud, clothes a little too tight, hanging out with a bunch of *blanquitos* with their J.Crew T-shirts and boxer shorts. It was scary and then there was Mark. [...] He was also going through a breakup with his girlfriend back home. And so we talked a lot. We would go to the movies, hang out at local bars, he even got me listening to reggae. Then one day we were watching the sunset by the lake. . . .

Migdalia Cruz

excerpts from

Dreams of Home

from

The Best American
Short Plays 1991–1992

SANDRA I am a fine woman. My kids loved me. I played
with them. I listened to them. But they didn't trust me. I
don' know why. I say that, but now I've said it. I think it's
true. I sewed all our clothes. They thought I couldn't see,
that I was color blind—but I saw everything. Only different.
I sewed a straight seam. I won a fair. I got a fine prize. Some
silk…I made a dress. It seemed a dress born on me. Like
my skin. They didn't like it. They thought it sealed me up
and I wouldn't have room left for them. They were scared
of me then. But they was wrong. I just wanted something
nice on my body, a dress to match my eyes—tight and small
and tired….What could be scary about a dress? They was
crazy.I am a fine woman. I have no more dresses. I wear
what I find. I never find dresses. People just don' throw
them out. You won't find nobody in this city throwin' out

their eyes. People like to keep those things. Those things are personal.

[*Pause.*]

I—I did see a dress once. But I had to turn my head from it....

[*Turns and faces front.*]

It still had somebody in it, but she didn't have no arms. Somebody cut 'em right off her....So...so I couldn't lift her arms over her head to take off the dress anyway. So I didn't bother. I jus' turned my head...but I thought if she only had arms then I could rob her. It was my color too. I would've looked like a queen....

• • • •

SANDRA   Even though we did it with our clothes on, it was good. I didn't feel dirty with this man wriggling inside me. It just made me smile. I can make somebody feel something for me and that was something. He felt real hot. Ready to explode with being in me. Ready to crack open my heart along with my legs. You sleep so easy now, like you went back to where you belong...and the truth is, you did. I wanted your wendell inside me since I accidentally fell against it when that crowd of nicely dressed people rushed toward us to get on the train. I rammed myself up against you so as not to fall onto those people. They call you things when you do that, when you faint or fall on them by accident. And that's when I felt that hard, little wendell of yours and I thought, "Hmmm, is this the man for me?" Is he thinking about me? Looking at me? I saw myself in the window of the train then and I knew you were looking at somebody else. Somebody dressed nice and smelling of perfume. But she wasn't the lucky one. I was . . . I got to feel your wendell on my back. I followed you after that. It wasn't no accident that I found you here on One-Hundred and Third Street. I knew this was a place for us to find love.

• • • •

LETTIE   I was born poor and I loved that. I had freedom. I played games. I liked playing in the park. I loved music. A man taught me to play the drums there. We played together all the time. We had four little ones. They were even poorer. I wondered what they were meant fur. I wanted them to stay alive, but got tired of watching them. They lived with my mother. She grew too old. One got past her. He went off the side of a bridge. We were sad but life goes on. And there's things down under the bridge, in the water, that needed him. That ate him up. He wasn't a waste. Nothing goes to waste in this world. There's always something to eat. . . . So I played the congas and stayed alive. My girls are good still. They get charity. They smile and then they get something to take home with them. They feed their grandmother. But they

don't give anything to anybody else. So I took a job. I ran a
sewing machine. It didn't play like the congas, but it paid.
People paid me money to make them dresses. I let them walk
on me. For money, I'll do anything. You can't be free forever.
With money, I could buy things...feminine hygiene
deodorant spray, feminine napkins, feminine shaving cream. I
could make a lady out of myself. I was so happy about that. I
forgot about my children; he helped me forget. We drank, I
worked, he slept...until I got to be too much of a woman for
him, too much of a lady. He said I lost my smell, the smell he
loved. And he walked into a needle and made me buy his
medicine. He was sick and I couldn't say no. I gave up all my
perfumes. I waited in doorways taking on their smells of piss
and blood. And other liquids spilled from broken people. He
left me then. I was too much my own person. If you get the
time, it's easy to know your own smell. It's the smell that
drives people away. Enough said.

[LETTIE *lies back down on the table.*]

Murray Schisgal

excerpt from

The Cowboy, the Indian and the Fervent Feminist

from

**The Best American
Short Plays 1992–1993**

ALICIA   [*Anxiously.*] Stanford, I saw Doctor Bibberman today. We had a truly rewarding conversation. I asked him innumerable questions and he was very forthcoming and...

[*A breath.*]

I want to apologize to you, my sweetheart. I was so involved with what I was feeling that I was totally blind to what *you* were feeling. Doctor Bibberman pointed out that you've been under enormous stress and you have *not* been having an easy time of it since you were let go by our mutual employers. It was as if Doctor Bibberman had removed a blindfold from my eyes and I saw you, myself and our precious daughter in a new and healthier and more optimistic light. [...] I admit, I admit, I was wrong, I was insensitive, I was cruel even. But not nearly as cruel and insensitive as Benton, Berber and Pollock. And I say this knowing full well that I started working there myself as a lowly secretary, your secretary, my sweetheart, my darling. You gave me my first opportunity, my first chance, my first introduction into the fascinating world of advertising, and today I'm proud to say, I'm second in line for Chief Merchandising Officer. But what they did to you, darling, discharging you so summarily after having served them faithfully for twenty-four years, half of that time as Executive Vice President of Creative Copy.... To discharge you without reprieve or redress during this awful recession we're having.... That was unforgivable of them. And even though I fought on your behalf, my darling, my dearest, fought with Ray Pollock until my own job was in imminent jeopardy.... I don't have to go into that. But I do want you to know how ashamed I am. I had no right these past few weeks, no right whatsoever to dispute or ridicule you about your desire to...to have a new life for yourself, whether that life be based in reality or fantasy. Doctor Bibberman pointed all that out to me today. He even brought up the subject of your deeply unhappy relationship with your father, how removed you were from each other, how your father never took you to a baseball game or on camping trips or passed on to you values that would help you achieve maturity. It may sound farfetched but Doctor Bibberman also spoke of your childhood games of *Wagon Train* and *Gunsmoke* and how they affected your decision to become a cowboy after you suffered the trauma of sudden unemployment. [...] When you left your first wife and your three young children to marry me, your secretary, an unsophisticated, callow, somewhat slovenly woman seventeen years your junior, a woman without prospect or resources, and when you took on the burden of supporting two families, sending our own precious Lucinda and your three children from your former marriage to private schools and then on to universities at great expense and obligation on your part, you proved beyond a measure of a doubt that you were a man of rare principle and generosity. And now that you're practically penniless, my darling, my love, my dear, dear husband, now that you're getting on in years so that future employment is highly problematic for you, I want you to know that I will do *every*, *every*, *everything* humanly possible to make your burden lighter and less suffocatingly oppressive. [...] I'll end my little speech to you by saying that it's my wholehearted intention to love you, love you, love you to death, and be supportive of whatever dream it is that gets you through the day. Doctor Bibberman feels that with time and with your continued visits to his office, you'll eventually disregard this...this fantasy of yours and return to a reality that we both can share and enjoy and build a happy, happy future on. In other words, my sweetheart, my dearest, you're not going to have any more quarrel or arguments with me, no matter what demands you make or how improbable your suggestions are. As an active feminist this is all very difficult for me, but my love for you is so complete, so enormous a part of my life that I will do whatever has to be done to make you healthy again, so help me God.

James Armstrong

The True Author of the Plays
Formerly Attributed to Mister William Shakespeare Revealed to the World for the First Time by Miss Delia Bacon

from

The Best American Short Plays 2008–2009

character

DELIA, a young American woman

time

The mid-nineteenth century. Evening.

place

An auditorium in the American Consulate in Liverpool, England

[*At rise,* DELIA *stands center stage at a podium. To her left is an easel with a placard that reads, "THE TRUE AUTHOR RE-VEALED." To her right is an empty chair. She is bursting with energy.*]

DELIA   Welcome. Welcome, ladies and gentlemen. I am truly honored that you have come to the American Consulate tonight. My name is Miss Delia Bacon. I'm from Connecticut; that's in America. Yes. I suppose you all know that, don't you?

[*Stops. Giggles. Returns to her talk.*]

Yes. Ever since I arrived in Great Britain, I have had one goal in my pursuits. To uncover the truth. And now, I am pleased to announce, that for the first time in history, I am able to reveal to the world the true author of the dramatical poems heretofore spuriously and falsely attributed to one Mister William Shakespeare. By the end of the evening, ladies and gentlemen, you shall know that name, that blessed name, of the true genius greater than all other authors. Now, before I begin, I must acknowledge the support of the man without whom I could not be here today. He has encouraged me in all my endeavors, and has even provided this lovely hall in the consulate tonight. He promised to be here this evening, so...please allow me to thank my fellow countryman, famed writer and American consul to Liverpool—*Nathaniel Hawthorne!* Will you come up here, please, Mr. Hawthorne?

[*Motions to chair.*]

Here's the chair, just like we agreed. He's right there in back. I don't mean—to pressure you. You could just wave or something. If you prefer. Will you wave to us, please, Mr. Hawthorne? Wave?

[*Waves. No response.*]

Mr. Hawthorne's a bit shy tonight. Pay him no mind, ladies and gentlemen. No mind at all. Though if you would like to come up...

[*Stops. Smiles. Waits for approval.*]

Oh. I see. Mr. Hawthorne is a bit skeptical about my ideas, but perhaps we'll convince him by the end of the evening. After all, your chair is waiting.... Well, I shan't keep you all in suspense any longer. I did have some notes here. Mr. Hawthorne advised me not to try to speak without notes. It's very important to be prepared, you see. That's what he told me. I just have to get these papers in order and then...well...Without adequate preparation, a speech is...I'll be right with you, ladies and gentlemen. Just as soon as...they were right here and WHERE ARE THE GODDAMNED—

[*Stops. Glances up at the audience. Smiles. Giggles.*]

Yes. Here they are. No, don't go! No! Please? Yes. Thank you. Sit down. I do apologize. I'm not a—I don't know what came over me. Well. Now we can begin.

[*Glances down at the notes. Looks up at the audience.*]

"Reason."

[*Smiles. Looks down at notes.*]

"Reason is the sole force which must motivate us in the quest for truth."

[*Glances up. Looks for approval. Uncertain. Turns back to her note.*]

"If we are to tear away from our attachment to the past, we must be willing to sacrifice everything, and head forward towards all the abundance that the future has to offer."

[*Beams.*]

We live in an age of progress, ladies and gentlemen, as I am sure our good friend Mr. Hawthorne would agree! As a matter of fact, if he would just...

[*Pats the back of the chair.*]

Well ... I'm not as good as he is at articulating these things, but I'll do my best. You see, the Elizabethan Age began a trend towards scientific investigation, and we must bring that same investigation to the greatest texts of that age. Only then can mankind, and yes, womankind too, be freed from the shackles of convention, which prevent us from ...

[*Quickly.*]

This is what *I've* been trying to get my brother Leonard to understand all these years. Of course he would just call me a— He could never appreciate it. Rationality. Why, if that scoundrel friend of his had been acting rationally, he never would have proposed and then— But I digress.

[*Smiles. Back to business.*]

Now if we are to determine the true author of—he *did* propose to me by the way—the true author of ... these most magnificent works ... it follows that we must first reject the spurious claims of that *man* from Stratford. Yes.

[*With disgust.*]

William Shakespeare.

[*Shakes off the name.*]

There are many reasons for doubting the authorship of Shakespeare, but three in main:

[*Checks notes.*]

"One. William Shakespeare was the poor son of a common butcher."

[*Looks up. Panics. Smiles.*]

Oh, come now, Mr. Hawthorne. I know what you're going to say. John Shakespeare was not a butcher per se, but a glover. But it's not much of a debate with you sitting out there in the audience now, is it? Why don't you...?

[*Looks back at her notes.*]

"Two. By all accounts, William Shakespeare led a sparse and altogether uninteresting life."

[*Turns back to audience.*]

An author of such distinction? Why was he not noticed?

[*Smiles.*]

Genius can only be ignored for so long, ladies and gentlemen. I myself have suffered from neglect. Been called names. Laughed at even! But it can only go so far. The human spirit is resilient, yes, but.... Sooner or later, one is noticed.

[*Motions to the chair.*]

Are you sure you wouldn't...?

[*Waits. Smiles. Giggles.*]

"Three." Perhaps the most convincing. "In light of recent evidence stressing the importance of heredity, it seems impossible that a man of such genius could be the only individual of note in his family." Why are there no other geniuses with the surname Shakespeare? More on this later.

[*Smiles.*]

If our author was not a man of the theater, what was he? I suspect...he was not much different from you, Mr. Hawthorne! A man of both literary distinction and governmental service. A man of connection to individuals of import. A man, perhaps, with a dissatisfied marriage, waiting to share his affection with—

[*Pause. Smiles. Sudden panic.*]

Or perhaps...this is reading slightly too much into the situation.

[*Smiles.*]

Ah, but, Mr. Hawthorne, do you not remember that noble sentiment from *Hamlet*? "Doubt thou the stars are fire....Doubt that the sun doth move....Doubt truth to be a liar.... BUT NEVER DOUBT I LOVE!"

[*Smiles. Recovers.*]

Now what at first appears to be a simple love poem, at second look, aha! "Doubt thou the stars are fire? Doubt that the sun doth move?" Is this not a challenge to the very foundations of a Ptolemaic universe? Why, if the plays were in Italian, we would have to concede they were written by Galileo!

[*Laughs hysterically. Pauses. Very quickly.*]

Yes. Now it so happens that at that time, a new philosophy was taking root. The mind that created *Hamlet* and *Julius Caesar* and *Coriolanus* also perceived this new mode of thought. The new philosophy, which we have adopted as a practical philosophy, not merely in that grave department of learning in which it comes to us as philosophy, but in that not less important department in which it comes to us in the disguise of amusement, this Elizabethan philosophy is, in these two forms of it, not two philosophies, not two new and wondrous philosophies, but one—one and the same!

[*Stops. Catches breath.*]

Well, what of this conclusion? Will it be attacked? Certainly. Just as Galileo was blinded by the forces of the Inquisition, I doubt not that a modern Inquisition is forming as we speak.

You know what they called Galileo, don't you? They said he was—

[*Calms herself.*]

I, however, cannot be silenced. And I can assure you, ladies and gentlemen, any evidence they may produce in opposition to my conclusions will not be of the least value. As for the internal evidence of the plays themselves, it is far too extensive for me to recount it here. I am at work, however, on a manuscript, which I hope, Mr. Hawthorne, you will condescend to read. Let it suffice for now to state that the author of the plays was none other than the discoverer of inductive reasoning himself, Sir Francis Bacon.

[*Smiles.*]

Yes, Mr. Hawthorne, Sir Francis Bacon. And yes, an ancestor of mine. You see now, I am not a *freak.* I come from a long line of great minds. Like yours. Perhaps you thought before that I wasn't worthy, but do you see now? So if you wish to . . .

[*Motions to the chair. Long silence. Nothing happens. Sudden panic.*]

But . . . could such a distinguished person, Sir Francis Bacon, allow his works to be performed upon the public stage? Upon the stage? Well, he wouldn't be onstage himself, ladies and gentlemen. Not sitting up there himself. But he would still support his works. What could a prestigious individual like Mr. Hawth—Bacon, have to fear?

[*Passionately.*]

Francis Bacon fought for a world based solely upon rational fact. Throw out Aristotle! Throw out Ptolemy! Throw out the Bible! Yes, Mr. Hawthorne, you mustn't be shocked.

[*Smiles.*]

Nothing should stop us. If we reject convention, if we put aside the doubts and hesitations that prevent us from seizing what we really want, we can create a whole new society. If the world were to see, if you were to stand up here with me and proclaim that what we have—

[*Quickly.*]

We can defy convention, Mr. Hawthorne. Traditions do not matter to us; marriage doesn't matter; forget about that New England cow of yours; I'll wear your scarlet letter! I may have gone too far last night, but you belong with me, not her! You were supposed to be here, Mr. Hawthorne! You promised! You said you'd be—OH DEAR GOD!

[*She screams and knocks over the lectern. Papers fly everywhere. She flings her arms in a mad rage and continues to shriek through tears. She stops. Opens her eyes. Looks out at the audience.*]

Oh. Oh dear. Well. I must say, I do . . . I do apologize. Where was I?

[*Tries to gather up the papers and sort through them.*]

No, please don't go yet. I still haven't gotten to the best part. You see, the plays are inscribed with a secret code. If you look at the sequence of words the second part of *Henry the Fourth* and count off using the square root of . . . It all makes perfect sense. Mr. Hawthorne? You are still out there, aren't you? You are . . . ?

[*Stares into the void.*]

I know . . . you couldn't sit up here with me. I understand that now. But . . . that was you I saw in the back. . . . It was . . . right? Mr. Hawthorne. Hello? Are you . . . ? Mr. Hawthorne . . . ?

[*The lights slowly fade to blackout.*]

Carey Lovelace

The Stormy Waters, the Long Way Home

from

**The Best American
Short Plays 2008–2009**

character

RENATA, late 40s to early 50s, beautiful in a wistful, childlike way

[*Empty stage. Sound of waves—maybe a foghorn. It is morning, a beach, very early summer; before it warms up. Woman comes over sand. Huffing and puffing, as if she'd walked a long way. She carries a basket.*]

RENATA   God! Sorry I've lost my breath here!

[*To unseen "friends" in the distance.*]

Come on! Hurry up!

[*Peering in the direction of the audience.*]

Oh. Hi! There you are. The fog is so thick. You got here before the others.

[*Waving offstage.*]

Over here!

[*A beat.*]

Hey! Listen.

[*A beat.*]

God, I love that sound!

[*As if struggling to regain her breath.*]

It gets harder every year!

[*She puts out different thermoses in the sand.*]

Okay. Barley soup. Juice. And this is *elixir vita.* My own recipe. Designed for anything that ails you.

[*Looking out, again, offstage.*]

I can barely see them. Can you? I hope he's okay! I get so impatient sometimes. I know I shouldn't. He's just so...you know! Slow!

[She smells in the different thermoses, pours out of one of them, offers it.]

You sure you won't have some?

[She sips, makes a face.]

No, it's great. Really. Full of vitamins! Listen, I need to ask you something. I'm glad we're alone for a moment. I . . .

[She shivers.]

God, a chill. Did you feel that? Like a ghost passing through the room. Isn't that the, what, old wives' tale? Old wife. I wonder where that expression came from. They never talk about "old husbands."

[Singing.]

"By the sea, by the sea, by the beautiful sea." You forget how long it takes for summer to come. I'm just so cold all the time now! I'm not complaining. Anyway . . . it's no use pretending things haven't changed a lot recently. Do you think I've changed a lot? Be frank. I want to know things the way they really are. And I know I can trust you. Can't I?

[A beat.]

Winter is still with us.

[She takes another sip, again makes a face.]

You know, there would have been a time I wouldn't be caught dead drinking this garbage. Give me a big, fat joint! Now I'm ready to do a cookbook. *The Power of Juicing.*

[*She looks in the cup.*]

Seaweed. See? Nothing better. Iron. Vitamin A. Japanese mystics swear by it. That's a nice sweater. Is it a sweater? I can barely see it. You're fading into the sand there! Whoa! Ha! Ha! Don't go away. Please! God, suddenly I had that...déjá vu. Like I've been here before. Do you ever get that? Anyway, what I needed to ask...oh, it's so hard. So hard to...I've been thinking about T. S. Eliot a lot recently. Do you read poetry? Does anyone anymore? "The tolling bell measures time, not our time." "I hear the mermaids calling each to each." When I was little, we had a house by the beach and my father used to tell me to listen to the sound of the waves, listen very hard, actually, to the sound in between the waves. He'd say, "Can you hear? That's the sound of the sounds of the mermaids calling. Listen. There they are." And I would listen. He said they were calling out to me, that they were sad, trying to bring back their life. He used to say I had hair the color of sand. I would lay my head in his lap and he would stroke my hair. I dreamed last night I saw my father. I had a conversation with him, the way he was when he was young. And then he turned into my husband. Then into T. S. Eliot. Then everything vanished; it was like looking through a telescope the wrong way. It's very weird, this whole experience. Suddenly, it's happening to you. I wish I could see you. Don't hide from me. You'd think they'd be here by now! Anyway, what I wanted to say was...I just wonder what he's going to do without me. You know, he's gotten worse and worse. He got so angry when he first heard. "Who's going to take care of *me*?" he said. He was right. It's been slow, over the years, and I never thought there would be a problem, because I never thought it would be me first, you see? He's still brilliant, of course. Have another drink of this?

[*She toasts, drinks, makes a face, tries to recover:*]

At first it changed my skin. That was the most shocking thing. To watch your body change. Fast. To look at your arm and have it be somebody else's. Then the loss of hair. You hold on to hope, some kind of thought it's going to reverse itself. It's incredible how strong that hope is. But, now, it's strange, I feel great! It's like I'm back to normal again! I'm afraid of the dark. At first there was pain. And fear. But then...it stopped. Are you there? They say I'm still beautiful. Am I? Always beautiful.

[*She drinks again.*]

"In the end is my beginning." I don't really trust Western medicine. But, frankly, Eastern medicine isn't much better. Wouldn't it be nice if this were a nice, fat joint? Actually, that's why I'm glad we have this time. I need you to...take care of him. I need someone to do that. And to tell people...how much I love them. Can you do that? Whoa! You faded out there for a moment. What did you say? What? I can't hear you. Can you speak louder? Please! I don't mean to be upset. It's weird, this feeling. Waiting for friends to arrive. Always waiting. Waiting for friends.

[*Slow fade to black.*]

Julie Rae (Pratt)
Mollenkamp

In Conclusive
Woman
A Multimedia Play

from

**The Best American
Short Plays 2006–2007**

time and place

Here and now

setting

Two projection screens, a vanity with chair, and a bench

text key

Regular Text: Spoken Lines

Italics: Voice-Over

SNAP: Finger Snap

Bold: On-Screen

VIDEO: *The Teacher* [On Screen One]; *Academic Strip Tease* [On Screen Two] *When we were naked for the first time, he looked down at me and said, "Okay, tell me everything." I love it when people talk dirty.*

Good evening, scholars. My name is Doctor Julie Rae Pratt. Hold a bachelor's degree, a master's degree, and a Ph.D. Have twenty-five years teaching experience in secondary and post-secondary venues. Published papers in prestigious scholarly journals and have been invited to speak at major national and international conferences. As a teacher, I strive to provide students with a comprehensive experience involving intellectual, emotional, physical, and spiritual facets, which contribute to their personal, social, and political development. These are some of the words and phrases used while teaching:

Do the work.

Wet.

Open.

Dripping.

Erect.

Hard.

Delicious.

Pink and puckered.

Open the lips wider.
Hair can get it the way but it's part of the fun.
Look toward the differences, that's what's compelling.
Butts are funny.
From a Midwestern matriarchal family, which the world saw as patriarchal, but we all knew who was really in charge. I was often saddened, even as a little girl, about the lack of equality in my parents' relationship. I can't remember a moment where they kissed, where they cuddled on the couch, where their passion was evident, where they praised each other, where they shared moments of silence, where they fought furiously, where conjoined in any emotional or intimate way. They were not partners, they each refused to give, they each lived out their lives together at odds. My father would fuck up and bring Mom roses and she would be furious because we couldn't afford them, she felt he did it to make *him* feel better—not to give her a gift. She didn't like *Flowers*, too frivolous; *Jewelry* too expensive; *Clothes* not permanent; *Household Items* relegating. That always stayed with me 'cuz I wondered what the hell she did want? I bet he did too. So why were they married? What did he see in her? A take-charge woman who paid attention to him. He was an only child. His parents were so in love with each other that he got left out. What did she see in him? Security, security, security. Her dad left. She was Daddy's little girl. He just left her. He had twenty-one other kids with seven other women. Her relations with men—you know what she told me? Never trust

them. *Never trust them. Never trust them.* They will fuck you over at every chance they can get, they will, they will, they will, they will fuck me over. *Forgivers need not apply.* She taught me to find strength in myself, and security in others.

These are excerpts from student evaluations received at the end of stupendously long, painful, glorious, bloody, exhilarating semesters: SNAP

"Julie has a way of pushing students to reach their fullest potential. From the very beginning she requires/demands student participation."

"She brought energy to the classroom and made us feel like we were learning with her and that what we had to say mattered."

"Students felt comfortable taking risks in something they have never done before."

"She creates a relaxed environment in which to learn, perform, and experiment."

"She applied her knowledge in creative, interesting ways. The variety of projects and exercises is very good."

Excerpts from student evaluations received at the end of frighteningly quick, wonderful, tumultuous, enlightening, horrifying goddamn semesters: SNAP

"Dr. Julie makes us work too hard, her classes are too intense."

"She grades too harshly, she's too demanding."

"The methods used to elicit answers were too forceful."

"The professor seems scattered and unprepared."

"Her classes give me way too much stress. Too much material, too little time."

"She tries to cram too much in."
Part of my self-definition is teacher. It's something I have trouble turning off, 'cuz I like the trip too much and because I can usually see...SNAP

The drain hole from my radical hysterectomy was above my pubis. It would have been obscured if I had a decent bush, but I'm blond—the tube stayed in me too long and caused an abrasion when it was taken out. Lost 9 lbs. in blood and water from the hole the day it was removed. SEXY! But that's nothing. The gastric bypass surgery—they made me a brand-new stomach by creating a small pouch at the top of the old, fat, never-full stomach. The new, improved, smaller stomach is connected directly to the middle portion of the small intestine (jejunum), bypassing the rest of the stomach and the upper portion of the small intestine (duodenum). Feel full more quickly than when my stomach was its original size, which reduces the amount of food I can eat. Bypassing part of the intestine also results in fewer calories being absorbed. This leads to weight loss. Truly. When your stomach is only the size of a circus peanut, the pounds just fly away like Dumbo. Try 120 lbs.! I lost nearly half my body weight. It's as if there were two Julies inside, and one just silently melted away. Sometimes I wonder where she went...probably to an all-night diner. Told only five people about this surgery. Because I was ashamed? Embarrassed? Conflicted? Scared? Or figured it wasn't anyone's fucking business. Funny how things change....

Of course, losing nearly one-half of me did some fucked-up things to my skin. Half of Julie was gone, but all of the smooth, creamy, pink skin that covered her was still there. And there. And there. And there. You've seen Shar-Peis, the Chinese wrinkled dogs? I felt worlds better, but I looked like a villain from that Dick Tracy movie—and I don't mean Madonna! Something would have to be done. Back to the knife! "Tummy tuck" time. "Okay, class, we're going to do head, shoulders, knees, and toes and then tummy tuck!

Audience Sing-Along

They removed a seven-inch smiley face of skin from my belly. They took the smile, the many pounds of flesh of my gut, pulled the top part down to the bottom, and sewed them together, leaving a flat belly, something I've never had in my life. The vertical scars above and below the fake belly button, unique for its pleasing heart shape, are from the bypass. As an added bonus, most of the hysterectomy scar was removed.

I've been 268 lbs. and 140 lbs.—140 lbs. is better.

But maybe not for the reasons you think.

Sixth grade, so I'd had my period for a year, and was fairly well developed. At eleven I had my tonsils and my adenoids out. Unspeakably ill, had to go back, hemorrhaged twice, had to be cauterized in the emergency room, it was horrendous and awful, and at the end of it, a month later, I had lost 25 lbs. and was actually too skinny. To make me feel better, my mom took me to the mall. This was the most frightening public experience I'd ever had in my life. The men would not leave me alone; it scared the living piss out of me. It was predatory—the male gaze and attention was so uncomfortable, so vicious, so obvious, and out of control that even my mom noticed my fear. She ran me out of there. Knew I'd just become the prey. For the first time, the prime target. This was the same year he said, "Ew, I don't want to do that anymore, what's wrong with you?" All that converged at the same time. At the peak of my adolescent beauty, rejected by the only thing I had known as normal, all this other pain appeared. But I knew how to fix that. I began feeding that fear right away. Sneaking cheese sandwiches, spending three hours in intense ballet class and then furtively eating a half gallon of ice cream.

Sneaking food. *Always, always, always.* Hiding it in my room, in the basement, in the car, in the backyard.

No longer wanted to be the prime target. I wanted back the power I felt before. I purposefully became a fat chick and used and enjoyed all the power of my size until that size threatened my life. That's what it took. SNAP

My junior high teacher—he loved me, expanded me, inspired me, sought and nurtured my gifts. He praised me, told me when I fucked up, laughed with me, held me when I cried, helped me learn and grow. Finally knew what it meant to be Daddy's girl. Hugged him at graduation, he pressed his stiffy against me. What the fuck?

My influence rarely extends to women anymore, when they used to be my strongest allies—before I was wise and jolly and, best of all, fat—they could take advice from me because they could lord over me based on my size—that's huge with women—"I love you but make sure there is something I have that is better than you." I'm

Thinner
Prettier
Smarter
Funnier
Happier
Healthier
Fertile

For some reason, thinner and prettier is best. But maybe not for the reasons you think.

I lay in bed with my mom. She still loves to cuddle. And she wakes up, looks at me, smiles, and says, "You really must meet my daughter Julie. She got a Ph.D., you know. You'd love her."

These are the little gifts that cut
And cut
And cut the pain.

These are more of the words and phrases used while teaching:

Satisfying.
Climax.
A good build is always pleasurable.
When you do it well, you'll be happily exhausted at the end

Afterglow.
Don't cut off the dynamite before it explodes.
Playing with others is more fun than playing alone.
But playing alone doesn't suck.
Get your ducks in a row.
Get your poop in a group.
Codify.
Silence is power.
When you hate you love and when you love you hate.

He and I would seek every opportunity to be naked together.
It was guised as:
Playing doctor,
Lessons he could teach me,
Giving each other a bath,
Sometimes with pee.
The ONE time I remember rejecting his advances was when
I awoke in the middle of the night on the toilet, legs spread,
he was kneeling in front of me, his penis in between the lips
of my vagina. He was peeing. It suddenly didn't feel good
anymore. It felt cold and wet. Was tired, groggy to the point
of unawareness. Began to cry. He quickly swept me up in his
arms, took me to bed, and held me safely for a long time.
Suddenly, wasn't alone, so not afraid. Felt connected and
even bad for not doing what he wanted. He drilled a hole in
the stairwell so we could watch each other in the shower.
That's when I first saw him cum. He was in the shower. Sat

furtively on the stairwell with a book in my hand. It was so
exciting. And it made me feel special. Still like to watch. Used
to feel guilty about it but decided not to. What turns us on first
is what continues to turn on us. The faces may change but the
act remains the same. Like to watch and be furtive and give
fully. Just as when I first became sexual. And THAT'S OKAY.
    My name is Dr. J. I have been observed kneeling at 1:30
in the morning on a kitchen floor surrounded by chanting
students as I sucked down a beer bong. *Doc J., Doc J., Doc J.!*
Are you familiar with beer bongs? A large funnel connected
to a hose connected to a mouth? It helps if one has done
various things over the course of one's life to diminish the gag
reflex.... Spit up the first time. It had been nearly fifteen years
since I had last bonged a beer. Which, by the way, was also in
front of students... and my mother. I have fed students,
individually, in pairs and in groups. Danced with them, cried
with them, laughed with them. Helped them get jobs, have
babies, go to court, get medicine and abortions. Paid their
electric bills, car insurance, and tuition. Created some good
and some not so good art with them. And taught them a few
things about acting, directing, theater, history, and
management, teaching theater, collaboration, and being an
artist with vision. Sometimes the learning happened on
purpose, sometimes it happened by mistake. But it happened.
They've cleaned, repaired, and decorated my house,
maintained my lawn and gardens, introduced me to those
they love, and come back to tell me of their lives. I'm their

mentor, their teacher, their friend, and one time, a lover. Students need to see that teachers are human and that they learn, too. Especially, teachers learn from their students. It begins when I THOUGHT I was five or six. When my mom and I talked about it later, she told me I was closer to two years old. My baby-sitter was the seventeen-year-old from across the street. He let me eat popcorn, paint on the wall with pudding, tucked me in with music playing. Awoke to him pulling my underpants down. The smell of laundry bleach was in the air and had wet sticky stuff on my back. Rolled over. He flew up, pants around his ankles, and left the room. Didn't know why he wouldn't play with me anymore. It hurt my feelings, so told my mom about it the next day. He never sat for us again. At six, walking home from first grade, a man in a car asked me for help. He wanted me to come closer to the car. Knew I shouldn't but couldn't resist the attention— he picked me. I must be smart. Or pretty. As I approached, realized he was playing with something in his lap. Surprise! Watched him cum as I stepped up to his car window. It was scary and awesome and frightening and horrific and fascinating. Walked quickly back to school rather than home. Albert Einstein Elementary was closer and wanted to be safe.

Unsolicited Advice
If you ever decide that you want to stay with her for the rest of your life, or at least for the next two weeks, these are some things you should think about:

You don't have to understand her, just recognize her.
Little gifts are a blast.
Do what you want and let her do what she wants.
Collaboration is fun, it's great to play by yourself, even better to play
with others.
Stroke her when you don't want to but she needs it.
Give oral pleasure.
Help her grow in the least mean way you can muster.
Don't be too lazy.
BE HONEST and KIND to each other, it's the greatest way
to care.
Become that united front against all forces, it's really cool.
Grow into a good daddy.
Go on adventures—grocery store, lingerie shops, hardware hatches,
pick
pumpkins and collect leaves and look at stars and take vacations and
SHARE SHARE SHARE SHARE SHARE.

That's what partners do. If you ever decide that you want to
stay with him for the rest of your life, or at least for the next
two weeks, you should do the exact same things. Plus learn
how to milk the prostate. He'll like it. SNAP

Mom has always been the Force in my life. Mom has
always been the Source that I draw from. Mom has always
been the Course that I cannot seem to chart. My mom's
biggest fear was not being able to take care of herself. She
often did it as a child, when her mother worked and her
father was gone. It was a great source of pride to her that

when my father left, she not only survived, she thrived. She is
PHENOMENAL WOMAN! Year one—When she began to
fumble, I notice. At fifty-two, she got a major long-term
disability insurance policy. That's when I knew she knew.
Watched her for five years before mentioning things to my
brothers. They retreated into total denial, the little fuckers—
men in my life often have the luxury of not dealing and that
exhausts me—they know women in our family will deal with
the shit and of course we do. My sister-in-law picked up on it
and we began the conversation—stories repeated, people
misnamed, taking too long to shop, working nine hours a day,
then ten, eleven, then in the office on weekends to get the job
she could no longer do well done. Not done well, but done.
Year seven—Finally mention it, she's horrified, remind her
that I promised I would take care of her, would tell her what I
saw, did that when I was in my twenties, at the same time we
agreed to take care of the other's pets if something happened
to either of us. So, mentioned it—denial, anger, paranoia,
frustration—she hated me and loved me more for it. Let's get
help, perhaps it's nothing, but we need to know. Was there in
the room with her when the words came out—Alzheimer's.
But we knew it for a long time before. Anger, denial,
bargaining, depression, acceptance—these were a whole lot
of fun.

Year eleven—She called the police at 4:00 a.m., claiming
there was someone in her house, they had been there for
years but they now were threatening her—Arabs and Negroes

and Mexicans, oh my. She was obsessed with everyone getting her. We kept her in her condo as long as we could. Belligerent and tricky, she had been hiding the disease for so long, she knew how to play it. It's a manic thing and so horrifying to watch. Then it's too late, she can no longer maintain after maintaining for more than twelve years—Keeping the secret—hiding the disability—not showing the weakness. All lessons learned.

I am Inconclusive Woman, woman, woman...
Able to hide pain in a single bound.
Performs herself powerfully.
Laugh even though her heart is breaking.
Pretends all is normal when her baby just died.
Publish two papers as her husband fucks around.
Makes others feel good when she is dead on the inside.
Acts like she's confident and she becomes confident.

Also a MILF. A mother you'd like to fuck but NOT spend your life with?

Every relationship destined to change profoundly as he or she dances out the door as all the little ones do? That ultimate goal of teachers and parents—to prepare them to leave and be free, not gone but not here. I will NOT be the consummate mother. Won't get to raise my own biological children—
Mommy, Mommy, Mommy! But do have the privilege of

editing the kids of others. And the best part of that is we get to play and they go home. And the worst part of that is we get to play and they go home. SNAP

At twelve, we decided to stay home sick from school. We wanted to play. Unfortunately or fortunately, my mom really was sick that day and stayed home with us. While my mom slept in her bed, on the couch I attempted with all my twelve-year-old wiles to seduce him. Finally, after looking up my nightgown for the longest time, he threw my legs back together, pulled my nightgown down, picked me up, and yelled at me. "Cover yourself up! What's wrong with you?" I knew our family affair was over. Our last sexual time together happened about a month earlier. We were listening to records in his room, lying on the floor. He pulled my shirt up and massaged my breasts. "This is all you can have guys do to you. If they do more, you could get pregnant. Be careful. Don't let that happen." He made the right choice not to fuck his sister. But the pain of that rejection stayed with me for a long time. And led to the desperate search for—and tremendous fear of—relationships with men. I know how much he loves me still. Know that he would walk through fire for me—know this. Just wish I didn't have to always ask him—wish he was just there.

Don't think my mom consciously knew about anything that was going on with me and my brother, but when there's that level of dysfunction in the family, you know something's wrong. Human beings can just tell stuff like that,

and women are especially good at it. Except my mom. She
loved, she nurtured, she cared endlessly—she just didn't see.
I knew she knew something was wrong, she just didn't know
what. She never asked. I never told. And now it's too late.
SNAP

I sometimes make points with knives so men will listen.
Are you listening? Used to have trouble getting men to listen
to me because I was small. Then had trouble getting men to
listen to me because I was fat. Now have trouble getting men
to listen to me because I'm a threat.

Unsolicited Advice
Becoming an object gets you attention—you become subject
for a while. Girls seek to be subject—we are taught that it's all
that is worthy. Yet, we're all both. And it's okay to be both—
being an object is FUN, hard, scary, being a subject is FUN,
hard, scary. They're just different. Balance is key here. The
idea is we're supposed to accept is this—girls are supposed to
show restraint, politeness, make logical safer choices. Bad
behavior = See You Next Tuesday, and we can't have that!
Boys can do awful things and it's not their fault; they can't
help themselves.

Well, FUCK THAT! When do I get to be out of control?
Take what I want? Push the envelope? Destroy some shit?
And be totally unaccountable for my actions? Boys will be
boys? Fine! But girls will be girls and we'd all better be
prepared for the consequences! SNAP

VIDEO: *Them Elmer and Geraldine Blues*

Men exposing themselves—at the store, at work, at school.
Obscene phone calls—where they asked for me before
engaging.
Accidental sodomy from a one-night stand.
Being thrown up against a wall by a student.
Being felt up in public.
Gay men reveling in my body because THEY WERE GAY
and I didn't exist as a sex object—their erections proved
otherwise.

Proud happy feminist, proactive, accomplished, loving,
joyous, smart, funny, caring, giving, giving, giving, giving,
giving, giving, giving! Not taking, not taking too much, not
feeling worthy.

Unafraid to ask for what I wanted but desperate for no one to
find out what I needed.

Unable to fully take care of me—but no one knows that.

Generous and loving to a fault.

In Conclusive Wo—fuck it.
     My female students are so much smarter than I was at
their age, and I'm so pleased. They still suffer the same

shit—oppression, being dismissed, mixed messages—but they evolve faster. They are amazing and I love to hear what they are thinking. Want them to understand that they are NOT the weaker sex. They are NOT the stronger sex. They are only and always who they are—and the potential in that is infinite. And that loving each other, not competing, not hurting, not undermining, not attacking, will ultimately bring them their greatest satisfaction.

Women are women's BEST allies.

Fourteen-year-old high school freshman—fainting and have migraines—one-week hospital stay with every scary test one can imagine—a borderline epileptic, they say. "There are two fuzzy shadows on your brain scan that we'll keep our eye on."

Inconclusive. SNAP

J.—first life-altering emotional love—gay: *140 lbs.*

R.—second love—celibate: *+20 lbs.*

N.—lose virginity AND broken engagement: *–10 lbs.*

A.—three-person affair with N. and A.: *–6 lbs.*

F.—gay: *+20 lbs.*

B.—black and beautiful: *weight stayed the same*

I'm a nineteen-year-old college student—have a lump removed from my left breast. Tell NO ONE. Drive myself to the hospital, lie to drive myself home. Not cancer but they're not sure what it is.

Inconclusive. SNAP

D.—engaged—my first orgasm with my first vibrator: *+30 lbs.*

I've since given over thirty vibrators away to my girlfriends—
my mother LOVED the rabbit I got her!

Twenty-one-year-old college graduate—summer—get
pregnant.

Six weeks on when I have an abortion.

Safe.

Clean.

Expensive.

Painful.

Legal.

Twenty-two-year-old high school teacher—winter—slip,
fall on the ice, and rupture five discs in my back—thus
continues the magical journey of surgical enhancement—spent
four days hanging from the ceiling. Doesn't work.

Inconclusive.

Play happily through my twenties with increasing
amounts of delicious fatness in my body and a back that is
tricky. Sleep with a variety of people—who the fuck knows
my weight? Dieting and gaining all the time. My back goes in
and out—I relegate pain to another part of the brain.
Sexual survivors are good at that. SNAP

G.—engaged—dumps me while putting the down payment
on our house: *+30 lbs.*

P.—a best friend—furtive sexual encounters he tells no one:
weight stays the same

M.—it was healing—she suffered a loss and I lost my father:
+30 lbs. Mostly happy—truly happy in ways others aren't

because enjoy the ride—find great joy in sensual
pleasures—looking, tasting, touching, smelling, hearing
everything.
SNAP
Michael—engaged—we marry. As I walk down the aisle, I
think, "Till divorce us do part."

Thirty-three-year-old college professor—one week back from
the honeymoon when I begin to hemorrhage vaginally—find
out I'm pregnant in the emergency room but the baby is in
big-time trouble—wait it out for five more weeks before I go
into labor and miscarry it—while teaching a class—expel into
the toilet, put it in my pocket and go back and teach for
another two hours.
Inconclusive.
Thirty-four.
Thirty-five.
Thirty-six—various "procedures" to help with fertility.
Scrape my uterus.
Blow out my fallopian tubes.
Laparoscopy my ovaries to remove cysts.
Undergo all these Kodak moments at teaching hospitals, so
there are tons watching the fun.
Fertility drugs, artificial insemination, in vitro fertilization—
tens of thousands of dollars.
The results are many miscarriages very early in pregnancy.
Inconclusive.

One of the perks of infertility is never having to worry about birth control.

Thirty-seven-year-old wife—260 lbs.—can't maintain a pregnancy. My back is in trouble again—can hardly walk and am losing the ability to do so as the nerves are slowly being severed by the disks.

Direct three successful productions, publish two articles, and am elected the leader of a national organization.

Thirty-seven-year-old hospital impatient—back surgery. The procedure has been 95% effective It doesn't work. *Inconclusive.*

Thirty-seven-year-old hospital impatient—second back surgery. *The procedure has been 96% effective.* It doesn't work. *Inconclusive.*

At 268 lbs.—can't walk and am literally going insane from the pain.

My doctor cries, "You're so young and beautiful," so I hold and comfort him.

Receive a teaching award and receive a major research grant.

Thirty-seven-year-old basket case—insurance pays for gastric bypass surgery.

This was the most painful surgery of my life but it's elective, so the drugs are fantastic.

Tell five people.

Hide the disability. Keep the secret.

Thirty-eight.

Thirty-nine.

Forty—getting stronger and looking good BUT learning new eating habits sucked. Having large friends and family treat me like a traitor hurt. Having a student accuse me of playing to the beauty myth made me feel ashamed. Husband has an affair with one of his yoga students. Tell no one because he won't admit it to me—he breaks the rules of our communion by lying about it—mostly because he can't handle my new body and the overt power that comes with it—power I've always wielded but now—it's more threatening because of the way I look. I forgive because the history of the relationship is worth more. FEEL BETTER and BETTER and BETTER And get pregnant!!! With twins.

I was going to have two babies. One for each of us.

Came home from school, laid out my grading, put on my pj's, went to the bathroom, peed, and wiped blood.

Put my hand down there and smear blood and tissue and know it's over—holding a dead fetus in my hand and my wiping has destroyed it.

Run and dress and drive to the hospital.

All the while keeping my hand sacred, sacred, sacred, sacred, sacred, sacred, sacred.

Am able to walk into the emergency room and calmly tell them I'm twelve weeks pregnant, which is when you're supposed to be safe.

You've made it to three months!

Show the receptionist my hand. They rush me to my doctor's office and sit and wait and examine what's in my sacred hand. The doctors appear and they run tests. And more tests. And more tests. Never stop looking into my hand.

According to the ultrasound, one baby is gone but the other is still okay.

Woweowoweowowowowowowowoweeeeeeee.

They keep my hand sacred until it's time for me to go home. Then the nurse says she needs to take what's in my hand.

I make sounds I've never heard before or since, growl and scream and bite and cry and lash out and don't watch as they take it from my hand.

My potential child, the one I'd worked so hard for.

My husband is finally there and he alone can calm me enough to leave.

Got to calm down because there's still a baby growing inside me.

But don't have a good feeling about it.

Within ninety-six hours, lose the other. Labor for five days—in CONSTANT PAIN but continue to teach and direct and deliver it on the toilet—put it in a velvet box and we say good-bye and it's over.

The autopsy showed both fetuses developing normally. The doctors had no idea why I miscarried.

It's (fall) SNAP

VIDEO: *The Vagina Song*

LOVED my big squishy body. It was fun and giggly and sweet and FAT. Jell-O has made millions off those qualities.

When I was alone, always naked. Touched myself everywhere all the time. Was soft and cuddly and large. In public, my Jell-O was raspberry with anchovies, pleasure with pain. It was sweet taking up space, and a lot of fun. Space is power. But it was also EMBARRASSING. People were cruel—*"Fat cow." "Fat pig." "You're gross." "How disgusting!" "You smell bad."* Even though I didn't—but that doesn't matter.

Outward appearance changes what comes to you in life.

There are rare exceptions to that, but exceptions are not the rule. The way we look on the outside is the way we are perceived by others. Had a certain amount of success when I weighed 268 lbs. At 140 lbs., my success doubled, trebled. The way I look opens doors for me. Lived on both sides of that big fat coin. And you know the craziest thing is I am the average size of the American woman. Size 14 and I'm still a fat chick.

After four miscarriages and an unacknowledged affair—begin again, Julie Rae. A new job with a promotion and a new family plan—adopt Ananda Rae from India—we wait for her until 9/11 takes her from our arms too—no international adoption.

Get pregnant the old-fashioned way—by celebrating a new house in every room—make it to three months and three weeks before announce it to colleagues at a conference.

Miscarry her on the toilet after five hours of agonizing labor—all by myself.

She was beautiful and lifeless and perfect and not there.

Begin using birth control for the first time in ten years.

Forty-one-year-old. I have a major infection. They can't identify what it is.

"Doctor, can you come here? I've never seen anything like this." Drugs make it worse—the infection actually eats the antibiotic and grows.

Inconclusive.

We await the birth of our biracial son—coming to us from a woman in Louisiana. Two days before I open a show, the Louisiana mom has her baby and runs away with him and a huge chunk of our money. Can understand why she wouldn't want to give him up. I GIVE UP. DONE. Never going to be the mother of a newborn.

The heart takes longer to admit it. Leave the nursery set up for eight months after the fact, then donate it all to a women's shelter.

Amazed at the amount of profound life experiences that happen to women in the most unglamorous of places—while seated on the toilet.

When men pee, they get to hold their genitalia in their hand. That familiarity breeds all kinds of power.

For women, it's a much greater challenge. You really have to work to see what's down there, you...oh, hell, you've all seen The Vagina Monologues and know it's worth it to

have a gander. And it often happens the first time while on
the toilet.

We *pee there;*
poop there;
masturbate there;
bleed there;
exchange information there;
find out we're pregnant there;
find out we're not pregnant there.

It's really a sacred place, beyond just being where one can take
a truly satisfying shit.

SNAP

　　She who used to provide three hot meals a day, sew all
our clothes, run a daycare, sing in a barbershop chorus,
manage a one-woman office arrived at our house with a
suitcase containing four sweaters, two pairs of pants,
10,000,000 pairs of socks, no winter jackets, twenty-five cans
of cat food, and a can of frosting. And we helped her, she got
better, we trained her like a newborn—to focus, to listen, put
on makeup, to dress, to do laundry, and she felt good and
useful and resentful and angry. She's so pissed about the
situation and we deal with that, she's so sad and we deal with
that, she's so embarrassed and we deal with that. The worst
thing for her is the recognition that at some point it won't
matter to her but that I will always know and be in pain
about it.

STOP!

More words and phrases used while teaching:

Suck it out.

Cowboy up.

Ovum to the wall.

Risk being naked—it's exhilarating.

Challenge authority.

Don't think like me—get educated and THINK FOR YOURSELF so you can engage with me.

Actions have consequences—be prepared.

Waves and layers are evocative—add more and more and more and more and more and more and more and MORE AND MORE AND MORE!

Push the envelope.

TAKE THE RISK!

I occasionally take my own advice. SNAP

"Assisted" living, what a comfortable euphemism—a bed, a bureau, a couch, a table, a TV center, we shopped and I picked it all out but gave the illusion it was her choice. It made it easier—practice fire drills, and locking the door, put the key around her neck, see her at breakfast or lunch and again after work so she can stay at this level of independence for as long as possible. She lives the non-life of assisted living and is unhappy. Begin taking her for walks as the weather warms up because I know she needs more care than assisted living but in order to move facilities with her insurance intact, she has to PROVE it by wondering off. Get her chipped and on the dementia patient hotline in case her walk gets her lost, she wears three pieces of ID jewelry because it's coming and want her safe. Give her the code to the door in song form— "1354, that's the way we open door." We laugh because "the" door doesn't fit in the rhythm. She finally does it, she walks out the door and to the lake we always go to and waits for them to find her, it takes under an hour. She gives me her watch—knowing that it will stop—I'm one of those people that fucks up electronic equipment—because it's time and she tells me to always know it was time and I did the right thing.

My mother is in a lockdown Alzheimer's unit, my mother is in a bib, my mother is in a merry walker, my mother is unable to walk, my mother is drooling, crying, laughing, sleeping most of the time, surrounded by glorious women and men who love her, make her safe, and take care of her, it's so lovely and awful, such a relief and such guilt. It's odd to hope your mom has a fatal disease so she can die, but sometimes I did. It meant her freedom and mine.

[*Look at screen.*]

Forty-one-year-old experiment—told there is an 80% chance of advanced uterine and/or ovarian cancer—a potential side effect of years of fertility treatments. Have a radical hysterectomy, not cancer—still almost die because the urinary infection left so much scar tissue that it began to meld my insides together—it wasn't a problem until it involved the kidney and the diaphragm and the bowels—all of the reproductive stuff just allowed itself to congeal into one mass—how profound—how *Inconclusive*.

I'm supposed to be flat on my back for three months— can't—have a job, a mother with dementia, and a husband who is having yet another affair. With a secretary. And he won't admit it—even after I find out. I ask him to wait, wait, wait and help me. Consult a lawyer and write my own divorce—served him the papers in black leather from head to toe on Valentine's Day—still have a drainage ball coming out of my gut from surgery, so put it in my bra to make my tits look bigger.

Two weeks after my fourth minor surgery in three months, go to court in a gorgeous blue suit and scarf, plead my own case, and win EVERYTHING! But lose one of my greatest teachers.

Live through it—the darkness gives way to the tiny pinprick of light. I know I'll soon be dancing in it.

NEVER ONCE met a woman who hadn't experienced some kind of sexual assault—not ONCE. EVERY SINGLE WOMAN I KNOW, EVERY ONE, and MOST MEN. Can I have a show of hands? Let's see if we can be a community. Any questions?

Unsolicited Advice

We've got to stop telling our boys they can take what they want. We must balance the privilege of boys and girls better, celebrate the gifts of each, cherish them, and help them learn respect and honor for self, for others. And to be kind.

Forty-four-year-old Barbie doll. What does one do when she is not going to have the family she planned, is divorced, and is taking care of her mother who has Alzheimer's? She becomes an adolescent boy. She takes those first baby steps into the hormones, she pretends she can live forever, she worries not, she takes major risks, she does things like drink too much, smoke too much, enjoy pot too much. She shirks as many responsibilities as she can. She messes with her career by taking risks, such as partying, among other things, with her students. She indiscriminately has sex with many, many, many people, and it's really fun. For about a year and a half. And then it starts to ring a little bit hollow.

[*Turn to a woman in the audience.*]

"You're worth it. You're number one!"
Women are not told that enough.

[*Turn to the man nearest her.*]

You're told that, aren't you? Have whatever you want. Expect whatever you want! Oh, don't shrink away from me. I'm not going to stab you.

[*Wink.*]

But I'm gonna think long and hard about it.

I AM the Surgically Enhanced Feminist.

My body is so damaged from all the surgeries that the insurance company pays for a tummy tuck and a breast lift with augmentation. It's really rather surreal to see your nipples sitting in a tray waiting to be put back on. 36D. I was supposed to be a C cup but

Inconclusive.

And as the body gets healthier, the vanity kicks in. What I learned in my forties is that the person I really need to be honest with is—(TA-DA)—ME! It is not better to look good than to feel good.

It is better to feel good because you like how you look.

You think I would have learned that by now. I teach actors, for Christ's sake. Theirs is a profession where 99% of the reason they get a job is because of the way they look. And 99% of them have to follow a very specific standard of beauty in order to work in most arenas. It's just the facts of life. It isn't right, so I battle to change the system from within.

SNAP

Forty-six-year-old content. Really happy. I learn that worrying is praying for what you don't want, so I meditate on what I do want. I receive the most intriguing message.

SNAP

Subject: Sincerely

I am 27 years old. I am a virgin. I feel you may be the one to teach me, goddess.

I e-mail back.

SNAP

I am a good teacher, Daniel. Tell me more.

Things said as a director:

Welcome to the circle.

I make the frame for the work and give the other artists the brushes to paint with, help their hands along.

Best idea wins.

Always know that I'm the queen.

And we create beautiful works together.

Bring three new things to every rehearsal.

Push, push, push, push, push, push, push.

Eat well—fruits, veggies, protein, and carbs.

Get sleep and water.

Plan academics and life well.

Work BEFORE you play—the playing is that much sweeter and burden free.

And Daniel tells me more—romantic, creative, emotional, intellectual, hilarious, hot e-mails—like a Civil War letter-writing courtship. And God knows I feel like I've been to battle.

We write—we meet—the first meeting is public with no talking. Just furtive, knowing glances and passionate forbidden kisses behind a closed door. He picks me up. I'm flying. My body is my art. It is the landscape that tells my story. And Daniel loves it as much as I do. We connect is profound ways. I am more me in his presence. I desire to be my best self, willingly shift with joy because it makes us BOTH happy. We're not perfect—but, man, do we have laugh! Soon, Daniel is no longer a virgin in a physical sense—and I'm no longer a virgin to partnership. He tells me he is the reward at the end of my journey. He is right. We marry. As I walk down the aisle, I know "till death do us part."

Our family.

And the dream that never dies, the wound that never heals, the ache that never left, finds peace. We begin the process of EXPANDING our family.

(Surrogacy) (Begin again)

We're currently in the two-week wait. Hope…it's a beautiful thing.

[Cross both hands and feet.]

I still don't know where I'm going. I just know I'm not going there alone.

Gained 30 lbs.

VIDEO: *YOU*

It's not the shit that happens to us, it's what we choose to do with it. ME? I work to stay open to the possibilities, be here now, laugh as much as possible, and enjoy the ride.

Unsolicited Advice:

Thank all of your teachers—from your family to your friends to ANYONE who touched you and pissed you off, laughed with you and hurt you.

Love everyone and they'll love you, OR NOT. Either way, you grow.

CONCLUSIVE

VIDEO: Sunset.

Laura Shaine Cunningham

Web Cam Woman

from

The Best American
Short Plays 2007–2008

one of five monologues collected by
Daniel Gallant under the heading
Five Story Walkup

[*An attractive* WOMAN *enters. She comes up from the theater aisle. Establish an imaginary door to her apartment. At the start, she is poised to enter. She speaks to the audience.*]

Hi. Come on, come home. With me....Just promise you won't tell. I want to show you something...private. Don't let on what you see. Here we are...2B. But you just watch from where you are. That's right—stand here, nicely on the welcome mat, next.to the mezuzah—not mine—it was here when I moved in! I didn't want to take it down! Hey, never tear down a prayer. Not that you're not welcome, you are! But you can't go in my apartment—you can just peek! Now, once I'm inside—this is important—don't ask why: DON'T MOVE, DON'T SPEAK! Okay, I'm in....

[She moves fast around the walls of the apartment, back flat to wall.]

When I talk over here...they can't see me. If I flatten myself against the wall, I am out of range. So now what do you see? You see me. And I look...perfectly ordinary...normal... right? Nice eyes, good trim figure—I work out! Tasteful dye job. Not from a bottle. From a salon. And my apartment— 2B—it looks perfectly normal, ordinary, too...an ordinary studio, rent stabilized, but stabilized too high, like a patient in ICU with a high fever—ha-ha. An ordinary sofa bed—it's cute, isn't it?—only $899 from Jennifer Convertibles—an ordinary coffee table, ordinary TV...ordinary bowl of mixed nuts.

Except for one thing! The seven cameras!

[She establishes the seven fixed locations along the ceiling.]

Camera one! Camera two! Camera three! Camera four!

[Gestures off.]

Camera five, bathroom! Camera six! Camera seven! They are trained on the center of my...very ordinary, normal apartment. Don't tell! Promise.

[She checks her watch. She slinks around, delivers following line downstage to audience.]

Men pay to watch me; this is how I make my living. I am what they call...a Webcam woman. I can't believe my good fortune: I just had to tell someone...who isn't, you know, part of it. Wow! They won't expect me for another five minutes—the mikes are not "on" yet...the cameras are always on...but...This is easier than going to the office. I was an office temp.

[*She slinks around the perimeter of the room, inhales to get less of a silhouette. To herself.*]

Suck it in, Suck it in.

[*To the audience.*]

Now, I just stay home and do what I do and it's permanent. And men, the video voyeurs, sign on—I accept MasterCard and PayPal—to watch me do...what I do. The trick is, I have to *forget* they are watching, or it isn't fun for them. I have to be...myself. I can...lie around on my couch, read the paper...they do expect me to masturbate, and—well—I do. I think they want me to masturbate more...it is amazing how you sense...this electrical "other"—which is, I guess, the "static" of their attention—I can never really forget—oh, yes, the masturbation—isn't it *boring*, waiting for me, maybe twenty-four hours, to start? And I can't get creative—it has to be just ordinary, normal, little at-home casual diddling, almost unconscious—not peep show stuff....I don't put on makeup, oh, maybe a little eyeliner, but no fancy panties.... But they never know when I am going to do it, so I guess that's the element of suspense in it for them, as I read the *Times*, or vacuum. I wonder—*how great is this for them?* But they never complain. They like that it is...natural. Hey, I am making $10,000 a month, I used to worry about making the rent, the Time Warner bill, the Con Ed. Now, I can afford slipcovers. It's fabulous. Isn't it?

[*She checks her watch.*]

Three minutes! I got to tell you something—[*She flattens herself, lower; we have the impression of a mouse running round the edges of her cage.*]—I had sex once, with a man, for them. The man didn't know they could see.... He didn't notice all the cameras. But something went wrong; he kind of...shriveled inside me, and...and he excused himself and pulled out...out of me, out of my apartment. I think of that guy, sometimes.

[*Upright again.*]

There are forty-nine of them. I know, of course, from the charge cards. They live in all the contiguous United States, and now I have one in Honolulu. A lulu in Honolulu. I am so happy and relieved that I discovered this new way to make a living. They pay so nicely: never miss. I used to have to get up and catch the D train by 8 a.m. to get to work by 9. Work, work, work—really dull, at the computer all day long. Now, I sleep in!

[*She dons a beautiful ivory white silken dressing gown.*]

They watch me sleep.... You know, it's funny—it disturbs...
my dreams. There must be something to R.E.M. sleep that
is...private, that doesn't want...to be observed. So my sleep
is getting light. Fitful. I dream I am...being not just watched,
but that men are chasing me to the edge of a cliff and I wake
with this yank—like being forklifted back to consciousness—
and I can't catch my breath, here in the notquite-dark I use a
night-light, so they can still see me—and [*She starts to crack a
bit.*] I get a little scared sometimes, my heart pounds and
pounds. I have them, the orgasms, the paroxysms, so many,
some nights, but after the first two orgasms they just get...
irritating. I know they are getting their money's worth. But I
get...no...[*She launches into the Stones classic.*] "Satisfaction...
but I try, and I try, and I try...and I try...." Until I am...
well, dry, and rubbed raw. This isn't how it's supposed to be!
Some of them speak to me—that's extra, but I will allow it.
They address me on the speakers. [*She points.*] See those little
perforated metal "mouths"—those are their speakers—which
I have to turn on in [*Checks watch.*] two minutes! 120 seconds!
They can direct my movements. [*She imitates a deep male
voice.*] "Arch your back." "Writhe." "Cry out my name!"
Confession: I don't like the word "masturbation"—it sounds
so...turbulent. You know what? I don't want to do it! I'm not
in the mood, even for myself! I just want to be alone! In
peace! Or to be with someone real, someone present!

[*She is starting to lose it.*]

I remember... belly flesh! Kissing someone's navel... Oh, those were the best sleeps, belly to back, arms... around my waist.... Warm in winter—I felt safe. I am not safe now, am I?

[*She checks her watch.*]

Okay. Mikes on. I can't be absent too long....

[*She flips the audio mikes on and slips the silken sash from her robe. She performs two skips, as with a jump rope.*]

I perform little fitness sessions, so they can see me work out a bit.

[*She playfully loops the silken sash around her neck, makes a comic gesture as if garroting herself.*]

But this is what you really want, isn't it?

[*She stares hopelessly out, the sash a noose.*]

This is worth, what, a thousand on MasterCard? PayPal! Only I never get to collect, do I? But... God.

[*She closes her eyes.*]

It will be worth it....

[*She addresses the cameras.*]

My name, my name was—Eva Marie! My mother named me that! After Eva Marie Saint in *On the Waterfront.*

[*Her eyes pinball, she is connecting to her true self.*]

No, wait. I don't want to kill myself.... Kill Eva Marie Saint? I want to... to get even, I want to... thwart you. And you! And you! And you!

[*She gives the fist to each camera. She pulls the rope away from her neck, cracks it like a whip.*]

You've ruined it for me—it started with the e-mails—why did I get those messages? "Enlarge your dick!" "Molly Bang Butt!" "My boyfriend has a BIG BANGER and I have a Tiny MOUTH!" I couldn't go into my own in-box and now you are in my own room, my inner sanctum—Oh, EFF YOU— I WON'T PLAY ANYMORE! No more CYBER MOLESTATIONS, if you please.... I want you to pay and pay and pay, and not ever get to see me do what you want me to do. You know what?!

[*She makes a mock punch, shadowboxing the cameras, one by one.*]

John! Larry! Mike! Ike! Gordon! Lionel! GEORGE!

You made me fulfill your fantasies... now you can suffer mine!

[*Music: "Someone to Watch Over Me" begins... softly. She dances, as if with a partner, dreamily, her arms around herself. She turns*

her back to the audience, gives a funny, "EFF you" twitch to her hips,
looks, smiles defiantly over her shoulder.]

This is it, pay pals!

[There is the sound of men breathing, from many men. Music:
"Someone to Watch Over Me." She is smiling, moving sensuously in
her solo dance for that "certain someone." Spotlight on her solitary,
ecstatic dance. Isolated spot on her face, beatific, longing. She sings.]

There's a certain someone, I'm longing to see...I know that
he...will turn out to be...someone to watch over me!

[Blackout.]

Neil LaBute

Love at Twenty

from

The Best American
Short Plays 2007–2008

one of five monologues collected by
Daniel Gallant under the heading
Five Story Walkup

[*Silence. Darkness. Lights up on a* YOUNG WOMAN *standing
onstage, looking down at us. A cell phone in one hand. Purse over the
other shoulder.*]

YOUNG WOMAN   "1-2-3-4-5-6-7-8-9-10-11-12-13-14-
15-16-17-18-19 and 20." Ready or not, here I come.

[*Smiles.*]

God, remember that, from when we were kids and you'd play
games, like hide-and-seek or crap like that, and one person
would be it, covering their eyes and counting to twenty or
however many and then you'd have to go find everybody or
run around, that kind of thing? Yeah…that was fun. Really,

really fun stuff. I loved doing all that, and being it, too, I never minded that. Uh-uh, I didn't at all, which a lot of kids never wanted to do—especially most of the girls I grew up around—because they'd get scared or shit like that, being alone in the dark or whatever, but not me. Nope, I didn't mind it one bit, being that person. . . . I guess I sort of like being the center of attention. A lot.

[*She laughs and stops a moment, checking her phone.*]

And I never, I mean, at that age, I had no idea how important that number would end up being to me. In my life. Twenty. It really, really is because I'm, like, practically that age now. Going to be, anyway, in a few weeks—December, that's my birthday. Not the whole month, obviously, but during it. On the 20th, which absolutely sucks because it's so close to the holidays that I always get screwed on gifts—"We'll just do it all together, on Christmas, and you'll get extra." My folks tried to sell me on that one when I was little . . . that I was so extra special that we should just pretend that me and baby Jesus had the same birthday, but all it meant was, like, maybe one or two more gifts than my sister got and not even anything big, 'cause my Easy Bake Oven (for instance) was the major package and my mom and dad'd just toss in a few other little bits—clothes, even!—and that'd be that. That was my birthday, which stinks. Completely. So, yeah, that's me . . . almost twenty. On the 20th. And what else? I mean, since I said it was such a huge deal . . . oh, yeah, right. This guy

I'm seeing, well, he's my professor, actually, in this one history course—it's my second year at college, so that's cool—he's almost exactly twenty years older than me. Yep. "Twenty years your senior," my mom says, which is so gay because she's only, like, twenty-three years older than me, but she sounds like my grandma or something...she always says shit like that, but especially about him. My boyfriend. Well, I guess he's not actually that, technically, because he's got a wife and all that—no kids, though—and that's a bit of a bummer, but he's getting divorced, he totally is, but they've just got a few things to work out. Legalities and all that crap and I've been very good about waiting for him. We started in together last semester—I'm only taking his "Empire Building from Napoleon to Nixon" because it fits my schedule and it's first thing in the morning, so he can give me a ride (my Honda is a piece of shit when it's cold)—but, yeah, we've been a couple for almost a year now, school year, anyway, and he's promised me that we're always gonna be together. Forever.

[*Beat.*]

Well, until today, that is. Like twenty minutes ago...

[*She stops and checks her phone again, then her watch.*]

Sorry...I'm waiting for a call. See, he just texted me. Dexter did. That's him—Dex, I call him—and he sent me this juicy message about how good it was last night and how much he adores being in my mouth and, you know, all that stuff…but actually, I was at Tula's last night, this bar downtown where I work—okay, dance—and I haven't seen him since Tuesday so, umm, that's weird. But the hurtful part of it is, the actual bad part of it is this: it's to his wife. Kimmie. That's her name— which really makes me want to barf whenever I hear him say it—not some other student or lady in town, which I could then understand because he's quite good-looking and sexy and all that for this older guy, but it's meant for his wife, who he is supposed to be leaving, and so that means he's lying to me, right? Lying and sleeping with her and all that shit that he's been telling me, assuring me is just not true. And now I know for, like, a fact…is. Yeah. Dexter's actually screwing me and Kimmie and God knows who else and you know.

[*Suddenly her phone rings. She looks out at us one last time.*]

Oh, wow. Here we go…1-2-3-4-5-6-7-8-9-10-11-12-13-14-15-16-17-18-l9 and 20!

[*Smiles.*]

Ready or not, here I come…

[*She lets it ring twice more, then goes to answer it.*]

Hello?

[*Silence. Darkness.*]

Peter Maloney

Leash

from

The Best American
Short Plays 2003–2004

character

CASSIE JESSUP is in her twenties. Southern. Cute in a kind of dirty way. She wears U.S. Army fatigue pants in a camouflage pattern and an olive-drab T-shirt. Combat boots.

set

An open area between rows of cells in a prison in Iraq. Industrial lights hang from the ceiling. Electrical wires hang down. In a corner of the space, file boxes broken open, files spilling onto the floor. Old office furniture scattered about, a metal desk on which sits a computer monitor and keyboard. Swivel chairs, some upturned. Against the stage-right wall, metal buckets full of water.

place

Abu Ghraib prison, Iraq

time

October 2003

> The Stranger is necessary, and antagonism directed against him
> has a biological basis beyond wishful denial.
>
> —Robert Ardrey, *The Social Contract*

> They wanted to know why I did what I did
> Well sir I guess there's just a meanness in this world.
>
> —Bruce Springsteen, "Nebraska"

[*In the dark, sound of iron doors slamming shut. Echo of men shouting in Arabic. Sound of dogs barking. In very dim light, a figure, silhouetted, is pulled to center stage from up right by a strap stretching off down left at floor level.*]

CASSIE   MOTHERFUCKER. Hey! Get back here, you!

[*Slam. Lights up on* CASSIE JESSUP, *holding on to what we now realize is a long leather leash. In her other hand she holds a baseball. She jerks the leash, the stops. She looks at us.*]

'Scuse my French.

[CASSIE *smiles, freezes, and there is a bright flash, as if someone has just taken her picture.*]

First thing is, you gotta show 'em who's boss. With a dog like this one....An' he's a big dog....Aren't you?

[*She jerks on the leash.*]

Yes, you are, you're my big boy. With a dog big as this one, see, you got to let hun know you're in control. At all times. He may be bigger'n me, but he knows who's in charge. Don't you, boy? Hey, hey, HEY!

[*The leash tightens and she is pulled off balance. With both hands she pulls the leash until she is once again at center.*]

That's why it's important you got the right leash. Thisn's nylon web. Tie-down strap I found up on Tier 2. Leather makes a good leash. It's got some give to it. Canvas is good. You can throw canvas in the washer when it gets all slobbery and disgustin'. Some folks like a chain, but a chain is heavy. Big dog, pullin' you this way an' that, you gotta ask do you want to add to the weight by using a heavy chain as a leash? Then there's your collar. Before you choose your collar, you gotta think about what you're tryin' to do. The purpose of the collar is to what? To *guide* your dog.

And when you got to, to *check* your dog.

[*She jerks on the leash.*]

Like that. That's called abstention training. Make your dog stop doin' somethin' he wants to do but you don't want him to. That's called negative reinforcement. Like a bitch snaps at her nursin' pup, he bites down on her teat too hard. That's a check. Hey, fetch!

[*She tosses the baseball offstage, waits.*]

You don't wanta fetch? I had this dog one time? Clyde? He was a mutt. All my dogs're mutts, purebreds're too high-strung. Clyde only had three legs. He was cool, though. Only thing is, he didn't like blacks. I had this one friend, Jewel? Well, Jewel couldn't come into my yard at all without Clyde goin' ballistic. Barkin', snarlin', just about pullin' the back porch off the house. We kept him chained to that wrought-iron trellis deal Tommy made for Mama. 'Course Mama wouldn't let Jewel come in the house. An' Daddy didn't want me goin' to Jewel's house. So I didn't see too much of Jewel. Hey, what're you doin'? Fucker!

[*She takes a flat, leather slipper from her back pocket, exits down-left. Sound of leather slapping.* CASSIE *returns, still holding the end of the leash and the slipper. She puts the slipper in her back pocket.*]

Gotta nip that kind of behavior right in the bud. Lot of folks say you gotta be *friends* with your dog, punishment'll backfire on you. But I've had lots of dogs and in my experience it don't hurt for him to be a little bit afraid of you. I mean, come on, who's the boss, you or him? Huh? Listen, *discipline* is not *cruelty*. That's my opinion. There's a place and a time for everything. Isn't there, Abdul? And this is not the place for you to do your business. Place stinks to high heaven already from all you dogs. What the heck would it be like if we let you make a mess wherever you wanted? Right. That's right! See, animals respond to *routine*, and one of the first things you gotta do is let your dog know where's the right place and where's the wrong place for him to do his business. An' we take you to the latrine, and what do you do? You refuse go. An' then what? We take you back to your crate and you make a mess and then we have to clean it up and we get upset, don't we? Or we don't clean it up, and *you* get upset. Either way, us gets upset, and we don't want that, now do we?

[*The leash has gone limp. She turns to shout over her shoulder.*]

Orin. He's smoked! He's tuckered out! And so am I! I think gone asleep! Or else he's dead.

[*She crosses down to look offstage left.*]

Not dead. Malingering. Take a break, Kasim.

[*She drops the leash, looks at us.*]

This wasn't my idea. Orin. Fuckin' pantywaist. Addicted to that air conditioner. I told him, you're gonna get sick you go back and forth between the hot and cold all day. Orin's from Pennsylvania. What's he know from hot? Says they got hot summers. Humph. Hot summers. Where I come from hot means you can't hang on the monkey bars without your gettin' burned to blisters. Streets in summer, you don't want to wear shoes with nails in the soles, 'less you want to feel like Jesus must've, walkin' that last mile. Hot ain't nothin' new to me. Doesn't mean I want to be here. Fuckin' shithole. You like it here, Mufasa? Course you do, there's no place like home, is there? No, sir. Yes, sir. Sir?! What do I do with this haji now? He's done his laps! Orin! Corporal? He's prob'ly chattin' up Remarque. You know Specialist Remarque, Kasim? Sure you do. You had her panties on your head the other night. [*She takes camera from pants pocket, aims it offstage left, snaps a picture. FLASH.*] Never thought you'd end up a screen saver, did you?

[*She puts camera back in her pocket.*]

He better not be doin' nothin' more'n talkin' to her! Fuckin' dog! I know he's a dog. But what can I do? He captured my heart, Abdul.... You know what? I'm gonna e-mail that fucker right now.

[*She rights a swivel chair; sits in it, scoots over to the computer on the desk, begins to type.*] "Dear . . . Corporal . . . Roper. You . . . dog. Get . . . your big . . . wet . . . red . . . nose . . ."

[*She turns to look offstage left, grins.*]

Thought I was gonna say somethin' else, didn't you?

[*She turns back to the computer.*]

. . . Out . . . of . . . that . . . bitch's . . . crotch . . . right . . . now. Or I'll
have you fixed! Arf-arf. Your ever-lovin' Cassie Jessup, PFC."
Ha.

[*She turns to look offstage left.*]

It's not fair, Abdul. This ain't even my job. I'm not MI. I'm
not even MP. I'm just hangin' here with Orin. I'm only here
at all because of him. He is my heart. My sweet . . . heart. My
only love. He fills me up like no one ever did in this whole
world. . . . And he' good-looking, isn't he? That smile? Oh,
he knows how to have a good time. Our last night in
Virginia Beach? Just after we got our orders? Shit. I could
tell you stories. Good God in heaven, now what am I
gonna do?

[CASSIE *turns front. She suddenly looks stricken. To herself.*]

Fuck!

[*She covers her eyes with one hand, cries. Recovers. Wipes her eyes.*]

Asante sana
squashed banana
We nugu
Mi mi apana . . .

[*Quietly muttering Rafiki's chant from* The Lion King, *she crosses
to the line of buckets against the wall.*]

Where's ol' Rafiki when I need him?

[*She lifts a bucket full of water; goes to stage-left portal.*]

Time for your shower.

[*She empties the bucket of water on the creature just offstage. Then tosses bucket offstage left. She regards her soaked captive for a moment, then goes to the remaining full bucket: lifts it, pours it over herself.*]

Yeah.

[*She sets the empty bucket down as she shouts.*]

Hey, Remarque! Get down here, you cunt!

[*She starts doing kung-fu moves in slow motion.*]

We'll have it out, right here, right now! Wet T-shirt contest on A-1! I'd lose.

[*She is at the computer.*]

Should I send this? Abed? Hell, why not? SEND. "Your mail has been sent." He's good at what he does, the Corporal. He does this same thing in real life, you know. Corrections officer. Upstate New York. Lordin' it over shitheads like you. I don't mean rag-heads, sand-niggers. I mean American niggers. We call 'em blacks.

[*She rights another swivel chair; sits in it. During the following, she may spin around in the chair; scoot around the room kicking her feet against the floor:* CASSIE *is deadly serious, but there is often something playful in her manner, even when she is talking about the most horrendous things.*]

It's all your fault, you fuckin' hajis. Everything was goin' good and then you had to go and do that. How could you do that? *Three thousand innocent people.* Motherfuckers. I got a question: What the *fuck* is wrong with you people? Huh? Do you think you are *ever* going to win? Do you really believe you are going to whip us? *Us?* Let me tell you somethin, Said. There's a creek behind my house back home. You know? Creek? Stream? Water? Like a *river*, only smaller? Anyway, it's a beautiful creek when it's runnin'. Lots of sunfish. Little fish? Taste great you pan-fry 'em. An' crabs. They're really crayfish but we call 'em crabs. In the summer th' creek dries up, an' you can jump from rock to rock and catch 'em in the shallows. Crabs are the fastest creatures. Little suckers scoot back under the rock they see you comin', so you gotta get' *behind* the rock and then reach around and under slow then *quick* snatch 'em up, toss 'em in the can. Well, we were down there crabbin' this one day, an' Clyde was with us. Ol' Clyde liked nothin' better'n the creek, and he's goin' nuts, jumpin' on the rocks, fallin' in, shakin' himself off, barkin' the whole time. All of a sudden, Clyde is barkin' like he's hurt. I look, an' he's in this one pool that's deeper than the others, we call it the clay pit. An' he's tryin' to climb out, but he's slippin' on the clay an' then he's goin' under. An' I realize that somethin' is pullin' him under' an' then I know: the snapper's got him. Big ol' snappin' turtle, you can go years without seeing him, but he's somewhere in that creek, you know that, but you forget it, you know how you do. So I call out to Walter the snapper's got Clyde, and he comes runnin' from a little ways upstream. He's been smashin' beer bottles against the lower dam there, but he comes runnin' when he hears me call. Walter's amazing. He's dead now, but.... He was totally not afraid. Of anything. He didn't jump in. He knew if he did he'd never find a purchase in that clay. What he did was, he just leaned over that muddy pool and grabbed Clyde by the forelegs up near his shoulders. Clyde was a big dog, but Walter pulled him right up out of that water, with the snapper still attached, his jaws on Clyde's lower right leg, just below the hock. An' Clyde is howlin' (he bit Walter twice, we found out later),tryin' to get away from whatever's got him by the leg. You ever see a snapper? Ugliest reptile ever invented. Prehistoric fuckin' monster. You think those IRF dogs are scary? We put a snapper in your box with you and you'll turn state's evidence in a *big* hurry, believe me. You couldn't tell 'em enough *fast* enough. But *Walter*, like he's in some science fiction movie. Walter grabs the snapper around the neck *with his bare hands* and just starts throttlin' him. The turtle's eyes are rollin' back in his horny head, tryin' to get a look at what's got *him* now. For a minute or two, it's a standoff, the snapper won't let go of Clyde, and Walter won't let go of the snapper. Clyde is howlin' and Walter's moanin' nngggg…nnnggg…nnnggg, an' I'm…I don't know, I was prob'ly cryin' about my poor dog, an' suddenly the turtle opens his jaws to try to get at Walter, not realizin' by doin' that he's lettin' loose of Clyde. An' then I'm holdin' the dog and Walter's draggin' the snapper by the neck upstream to the dam. There's all these rusty wires and rods stickin' outa the concrete and he wraps this piece of wire around the snapper's neck and hangs him up there on the dam. When we get back from takin' Clyde to the vet's, the turtle's still alive, scratchin' at the concrete, tryin' to push off from the dam with his flippers. But he wasn't goin' no place. Me an' Walter took turns throwin' rocks at the bastard. Hittin' him with sticks. Broke his shell all to shit. Took three days for him to die. We left him hangin' there, stinkin' in the sun. Flies had a field day. Clyde lost his leg. But he lived a good long time with just the three. He was a good ol' dog. What's my point here? Do I have a point? I don't know. Maybe it's…Maybe it's that snappers are strong…an' nasty…an' tough. But they're dumb. An' they're not as strong as Walter.

[CASSIE *puts her hand on her belly.*]

I don't feel so good.

[*She mumbles Rafiki's chant to herself.*]

Asante sana squash banana…Orin!…Come get this guy!
He's softened up.

[CASSIE *suddenly moves to the bucket she emptied over herself,
drops to her knees, vomits into it. Her back to us, we see her muscles
contracting, relaxing, contracting, hear wrenching sounds as she
pukes hard into the metal pail. Finally, the retching and she rests, her
head still in the bucket. Quiet moans. She lifts her head, turns wiping
her mouth with her forearm. Wet dripping from her mouth, eyes,
and nose. Wasted, she sits on the swivel chair, leans forward, her head
in her hands. After a moment, she raises her head, looks offstage left.*]

I got a question.

[*She takes a folded, laminated card from her pocket, unfolds it, finds
the phrase she's looking for; reads.*]

Fee 'indi suaal.

[*There is no response. She looks up and offstage left, then looks down
at the card, looks for a phrase, finds it, looks up again.*]

Aeish ismak.

[*There is no response.*]

What is your name?

[*There is no response.* CASSIE *folds the card, puts it in her pocket,
turns front.*]

I didn't come here of my own accord. And I can't leave that way.

[*She takes the camera from her pocket.*]

Whoever brought me here will have to take me home.

[*She lifts the camera, aims it at us.*]

Inshallah.

[*She takes our picture. FLASH.*]

Polly Frost and Ray Sawhill

The Last Artist in New York City

from

The Best American
Short Plays 2008-2009

AUTHORS' NOTE:

We intend this play to be specific to the circumstances of its production. Thus, the name of the theater space in which this play will be performed in your production should be substituted for "PS 122," and the name of the actor who will be performing the main role in your production should be substituted for "Karen Grenke." (Karen acted in the first production of this play, which took place at PS 122.) We are also open to other substitutions for "New York City" and for the suburb "Metuchen" as long as we are consulted and give our agreement prior to performance.

scene one

Metuchen Mall

ANNOUNCER VOICE   Ladies and gentlemen, as the last performance at PS 122 before Chase/Wachovia–Whole Foods moves in for your financial and shopping ease, Theatre Askew presents Karen Grenke, "The Last Artist in New York City."

[KAREN *is moving into the theater space with a flashlight. Points it at walls, ceiling, people in the audience, at herself.*]

KAREN   [*To audience.*] Walking through the Metuchen Mall.... By my side, Xavier, my former lover in the Polyamory Art Collective.... You may know them as PAC.... Years ago, Xavier helped me find my current style.... Of course I helped him equally.... Metuchen, you ask? Central Jersey is the answer.... Central Jersey is always the answer.... My old partners had abandoned Williamsburg years ago....

[*Flashlight continues picking out things. To audience.*]

Dark corridors...dried-up fountains...display windows for Linens Etc. and Williams-Sonoma now cracked and jagged....Sullen kids in tight pants and spiky hair camping out and smoking....We're inside an abandoned mall, but I'm reminded of photos I once saw in a book about Astor Place in the '70s.... Xavier is talking.

[*As* XAVIER.]

Why has it taken you so long to visit us in person? The time has come for you to give up the big city dream. Baby, New York doesn't care about art anymore.

[*To audience.*]

Xavier pushes open a huge door.... Rave music up. People dancing, flashing lights, pulsing electronica....

[*To* XAVIER.]

Oh my God, Xavier, this is the greatest scene ever, Retro-Hindu-Trance, aren't I right?

[*As* XAVIER.]

Welcome to the Big Box, baby.

[*To audience.*]

When the day began I had no idea how momentous it would prove.

[*Rave music continues for a few seconds, then stops.*]

scene two

Karen on Segway

[*Swirly pink-green light. Earlier that day. Hurrying between jobs.* KAREN *quaffs Red Bull.*]

KAREN   [*To audience.*] Floating through the city on my faithful Segway.... Between one job and the next.... Five day jobs and I barely get by.... Bouncing.... Ah, the hallowed cobblestones of SoHo.... Paying tribute.... The greats of the past... Karen Finley, Eric Bogosian, Spalding Gray... Then through Chelsea.... Once full of galleries, now playdate central for families.... In midtown, the former sites of Sonnabend, Castelli, Pace Wildenstein.... I nod silently.... Wavy... blue glass... high-rises... taking over everywhere.... I hate those fucking things!

[*Ka-hoop of iPhone e-mail notification interrupts.* KAREN *tries to keep balance as she pulls out iPhone and calls up e-mail.*]

[*To audience.*]

Stefani Symonds. Dot N-Y Times? That's right, the *Times.* The *New York* fucking *Times!* She wants to do a feature. That's right, about me, Karen Grenke. "You're the last remaining artist in New York City. You're a cultural landmark." Omigod, omigod, omigod.... After all these years…all my sacrifices…my time as a New York artist has finally come!

[*Twirls around on Segway in joy and—horn honks—almost gets run over.*]

scene three

Karen at Frank Gehry High

[*Hard white light up. KAREN is at desk in "teacher" mode—think Spalding Gray in eyeglasses. Takes a big swig of Red Bull.*]

KAREN   [*To audience.*] There I was, behind my teacher's desk, at Frank Gehry High for the Developmentally Gifted on the Upper East Side. As my students settled in, I crafted a proud e-mail to my former mates in the Polyamory Art Collective…PAC.…Been years since I last wrote them. But I felt certain they'd be happy for me.…The great artistic spirit that this city once had…embodied now in me and me alone!…I was still buzzed as I began talking about Warhol's immortal brilliance.

[*As student.*]

Screw immortality. How'd his paintings do at the most recent auction?

[*To audience.*]

God, how I hated these new entitled brats! But it was my own fault, I was the one who'd persuaded the principal to let me replace Introductory Art History with Art as Recession Investment Strategy. It was time to steer the conversation in a productive direction.

[*To class.*]

Hey, I have a fun announcement this morning. The *Times* is doing a feature on me. That's right, me, your very own teacher, Ms. Karen Grenke. You never really believed I was an artist, did you? But now—

[*As student.*]

What's the *Times*?

[*To class.*]

You really don't know? It's what we used to call a major news source. It symbolized New York and its great cultural life.

[*As student.*]

Losing strategy. The underlying mortgage on that new Renzo Piano building is killing them. You should be targeting Collegehumor.com instead.

[*To audience.*]

Christ! After class, I was unlocking my Segway. I noticed this shy girl from class standing there. You know the type. Gaunt...dreamy...her hair a different color every week.

[*As* JESS.]

Sorry about my idiot classmates. Screw them. They know nothing about art.

[*To* JESS.]

Oh. And you do?

[*To audience.*]

She pulled out her iPhone....It's a YouTube mash-up showing Schnabel, Fischl, and Sherman mouthing the lyrics to "Sheena Is a Punk Rocker."

[*As* JESS.]

I did it by myself. After Effects. Flash. Final Cut.

[*To audience.*]

I started to lecture her about giving people you're stealing from credit, then...decided not to go there. Why squash creativity?

scene four

Karen on Segway

[*Lights change back to Segway-swirly.* KAREN *on Segway, a dreamy-pleased state, slurping Red Bull as she steers with one hand.*]

KAREN   [*To audience.*] So there's hope.... New York may have a cultural future after all.... Cruising home... me and my Segway merging as one.... Crossing 14th... ah, my beloved East Village... home of the Beats... the punk rock revolution....

[*Takes big swig of Red Bull. It has its effect.*]

But even downtown the bio-morphing blue glass buildings are taking over.

[*Another big swig.*]

Fuckers!

[*iPhone e-mail goes ka-thump.* KAREN *calls it up.*]

[*To audience.*]

Eden, my rival for Xavier in the Polyamory Art Collective... PAC.... I know what you're thinking—"rivalry"? Well, if you're polyamorous you know how it goes.... All the blah-blah around who's sleeping with who.... Ethical sluts talk more than they fuck.... But there was just no getting past our feelings of possessiveness....In the space behind Eden, the other members of PAC writhe in a naked heap....Rehearsal or orgy?

[*As* EDEN.]

Congrats! We'd help you celebrate in person but we never come to NYC any longer. Honey, today's real artists don't even know where Manhattan is.

[*To audience.*]

Once a bitch, always a bitch? Why can't Xavier see that!

[*Swigs Red Bull in fury.*]

scene five

Karen at her Apartment

[*Swirly lights stop.* KAREN *now sitting on the desk, as though on sofa or bed. Empty cans of Red Bull in a mess around her.*]

KAREN   [*To audience.*] The real trouble, I was starting to realize—I've been so busy maintaining life in New York that I haven't gotten much art done. None. Zero. Nada. What will I have to show when I meet with Stefani?

[*Takes big swig of Red Bull. Sets empty can down among others. Contemplates arrangement of cans. Rearranges them. To self.*]

I was starting to see some real artistic possibilities....

[KAREN *kisses the Red Bull. Fondles it. Runs the can of Red Bull over arms,, head, legs, boobs, tummy. Starts to masturbate using the can of Red Bull. In big gesture of heedlessness, she sweeps all the other cans of Red Bull onto the floor. As she's starting to feel the heat—the iPhone makes its e-mail ka-thunk sound.*]

Oh shit!

[KAREN *calls up e-mail. To self.*]

Say it isn't so!

[*To audience.*]

Stefani's been downsized. The underlying mortgage really is causing hell at the *Times*! And worse—the article about me is off! What has my life been about!? I blasted off a woeful mass message to my entire e-mail list. The Collective got back to me instantly....

scene six

Karen on Segway

[*This time we get a nightmare version of swirly pink-green Segway lighting and subjective movement. It's dark and stormy, and KAREN is despairing.*]

KAREN   [*To herself and the audience.*] Come join us, they
say.... A performance in Metuchen, they say.... It's the old
loyalties that help us out in tough times.... I throw on my old
art-block party clothes.... The first time in years.... The
Segway and I are off.... Dodging potholes.... Steering around
young families with their damn baby strollers.... Blind with
emotion, we fly—fly!—through the rain.... Screw you, New
York City.... Screw your SUVs...your endless bank
branches.... I hate tourist-safe neighborhoods.... Screw your
K-Marts...your Barnes and Nobles...your family-friendly
Disney musicals.... I hate branding!... Trader Joe's I'll make
an exception for.... Excellent prices on wine...and like that—

[*Lights go to black. Big whoosh sound.*]

[*To audience.*]

I was in the tunnel on my way to central Jersey.

scene seven

Metuchen Mall

[*Flashlight in* KAREN's *hand, as in opening scene. Sounds of flogging
and moaning.* KAREN *stares offstage, takes big swig of Red Bull.*]

KAREN   [*To audience.*] In a room to one side of the dance
space Xavier is laying into Eden...when I was living with the

Collective, flogging and suspensions weren't our thing. But
ever since Kink.com took all those awards for BDSM porn
everyone has been into it.... Ouch!... Still—oh, Christ, look
at that.... So gruesome.... It really is beautiful.... Shit, that
was a motherfucker of an orgasm.... I have to say that PAC is
doing their best work ever.... Hanging exhausted from the
rack, Eden is transformed into an icon of desire.... No! No! I
can't keep watching.... Artistic jealousy.... Sexual jealousy....
It's a lethal combination! . . .

[*Rave lighting and music up as* KAREN *switches off flashlight and
staggers back to desk. Starts to climb stairs up to desktop but she's so
emotional that she stumbles. A strobe light pops off.*]

What the hell?

[*Looks around. Another strobe pops off, then another.*]

[*To herself and the audience.*]

Somebody shooting photos.... Right up between my thighs!

[*To stranger.*]

Hey, quit it!

[*To audience.*]

A woman. At least it isn't some pathetic frat boy.... We gasp.
We look at each other in confusion.

[*To stranger.*]

I know you ! You're Stefani Symons!

[*As* STEFANI.]

Karen, I'm sorry that the story didn't—

[*To* STEFANI.]

And I'm sorry about your job.

[*As* STEFANI.]

Don't be. I landed a gig with Collegehumor.com two hours later. Between us, the *Times* is going to be bought out by Collegehumor.com within the month anyway.

[*To audience.*]

Stefani snaps a couple more shots. . . . She promises to put them on College Humor's site later in the evening. . . . Screw it. If I'm going to be here at all I should dance, damnit, dance . . . I give over to the wild spirit around me. . . . Pouring vodka into my Red Bull. . . . In the ladies' room taping on smart-drug skin patches. . . . Maybe I do need to throw aside my dreams. . . . Maybe it's time to move to Jersey. . . . The stall door swings open—it's Xavier. He glares at me. "Fuck polyamory," I mouth at him. . . . Ten minutes later I'm leaning against a wall. . . . Groups of people—anyone passing by—is writing on my legs, my back, my arms. . . . I'm being inscribed. . . . Someone is drawing on my tummy. A girl with pink hair stands up.

[*As* JESS.]

Ms. Grenke, please don't tell my parents you saw me here.

[*To audience.*]

It's Jess, the arty girl from Frank Gehry High!

[*To* JESS.]

How'd you know about this scene?

[*As* JESS.]

Everybody knows Metuchen is where it's at. I get out to the Big Box every week. I take the bus and change into my party clothes at the Metuchen bus station. God, it's so depressing to have to live in Manhattan! Did you see what I wrote on your left arm?

[*To self.*]

"You are my role model."

[*To* JESS.]

Really?

[*To audience.*]

We share a big hug. Jess looks deep into my eyes. We're naked to each other emotionally, spiritually, artistically. Then she can't help herself and bolts.

[*As JESS.*]

I gotta get home to boring Manhattan. But I admire you so much I'm gonna write about how great you are on my blog. I get tons of hits!

[*Calling to* JESS.]

Sweetie, I haven't done any art in four years!

[*As* JESS.]

Don't you know what you are to me? What you represent? Check out your other arm!

[*Reads writing on the arm.*]

"Karen Grenke has stayed in New York. That is the performance. You are the art."

[*Inspired,* KAREN *waves bye-bye to* JESS, *then climbs stairs to desktop as music gets louder.*]

[*To self, audience.*]

I am my own art form. My life...My art....

[*Up on the desk now, music gets louder; KAREN dances.*]

[*To audience.*]

Okay, so immortality isn't in the cards. That dream is dead. But tomorrow I'll be the last artist in New York City once again And I'll be showing up on College Humor, and on a very cool girl's blog.

[*Pulls string attached to large can of Red Bull mounted on ceiling. Glitter falls from it all over her.*]

[*To audience.*]

There's always the chance that I could go viral!

[*Dances ecstatically, finally released.*]

scene eight

[*Music fades, house lights come up. KAREN shifts back into being "herself," awkwardly getting down off desk and picking up a stack of flyers.*]

KAREN   [*To audience.*] Thank you very much for watching my performance.

ANNOUNCER VOICE   [*Interrupts.*] Thank you for joining us at this final show at PS 122.

[KAREN *waves to stage manager to shut the announcer up, but construction crew guys are coming onstage to initiate demolition. KAREN gives them an outraged look, hurries to audience, and starts handing out her flyers.*]

Join me on May 16, 2019, at 10 p.m. for a talk-back about the important issues that I've raised in this piece! Will there be any art at all in Manhattan by that time?

ANNOUNCER   Please ignore the artist and begin filing in an orderly fashion out the doors so that the construction crew can begin the transformation of this ratty disgrace of a building into a gleaming new retail space—

KAREN   We'll be meeting on the comer just outside no matter what blue glass piece of shit the fuckers have turned this building into! Please show up and help celebrate our legacy! Help me do it so that art will not be forgotten!

ANNOUNCER   Be sure not to forget your personal belongings, and remember to return to enjoy Chase/Wachovia–Whole Foods, a new concept in banking/shopping pleasure, designed from the bottom up to suit you, and the way you tell us that you like to live....

Pamela Sneed

Kong

from

The Best American
Short Plays 2005–2006

Kong—Part 1

Hands folded
Head down
Shoulders slouched
which I've told my students in the University to never do
but that was at a time when I earnestly believed
and I now I stand here wearing big Dumbo ears
a pig snout
carrying shards of a broken heart
looking like a cartoon character in a medieval play
because I earnestly believed
but before I go there
I want to talk about that last *Star Wars* movie which
they promised was a final installment
But we'll see

all I can say is it really sucked
except for the part near the end
where you see the transformation of Luke Skywalker's dad
    Anakin
into the evil Darth Vader
His innocence destroyed
crawling through some molten lava—limbless
He looked like a soldier
or something out of a war movie
one of those battered survivors
who has left his child self behind him
But, I earnestly believed
And now all I can do is carry myself/battle scarred
to some semblance of safety
All I can do is hold on like a survivor of the tsunami tidal wave
Hold on to a tree, a pipe, anything, my papers from an
old life
verifying who I am
wait for the storm to pass
a shoulder to lean on/anything
But I earnestly believed.
You know when I left my parents' house
the small town for a big city
and experienced all accoutrements of a counter culture
I earnestly believed
queer boys
queer nations

nose rings
dread locks
muscle shirts on girls
dykes with nipple rings
punk rockers
were all some semblance of an alternative
I believed poet Glen James
who called us the sissified warriors
I believed when Marlon Riggs premiered the groundbreaking
    film
for Black Gay Men, *Tongues Untied.*
I believed Audre Lorde when she said in synopsis if we
don't do our work
One day women's blood will congeal upon a dead planet.
I believed poet Assotto Saint in all 6 ft. 4 of his cross
dressing self
I believed when he stood up at the funeral of Donald
Woods
and said in essence we must tell the truth about who
we really are.
I believed Black lesbian writer Pat Parker when she declared
straights are okay, but why must they be so blatant
I earnestly believed when my child eyes almost twenty
years ago
first saw bisexual poet June Jordan
and the first thing she said was this country needs a
revolution.

I believed when I first read Christos, the Lesbian Native
    American author of *Not Vanishing* and *Dream On*
when she wrote of AIM, the American Indian Movement,
    and said
"when I first heard you'd surrendered you don't know how
    much
I needed for you to go on."
I believed ten–fifteen years ago when the Hetrick-Martin
Institute for queer youth
was still just a one- or two-room shack
located on the Westside Highway across from the piers
and no one invested in our lives
I believed even as an almost child working in that
agency
when many of us who pioneered were like slaves,
singularly doing the work
of twenty, thirty people
I believed in Nelson and Winnie premiering even at the
height of apartheid with their fists
and heads held high
I believed before Jennifer, Jessica whatever her name
is on *The L Word*.
I believed even after they found Angel my student at
Hetrick-Martin murdered
a handsome boy chopped into pieces
Yeah when they were still pulling queers out of the
river there downtown

Dead from queer bashings and suicide
And then Kiki another bright young black queer
was murdered in the Meat District
Before him was Marsha P. Johnson, a drag queen and
    neighborhood fixture
bashed and thrown into those waters
Even after they buried brethren artists and poets,
Essex, Rory, Don, Donald, Craig, Alan
And cancer got Audre, June and Pat Parker
I kept on believing change was possible.
I read the literature
had hope
I lived in America after all.
I've sort of joined the middle class.
I believed when I first saw a woman's silhouette in
5 a.m. light.
I believed kissing her nakedness
there'd be honor there.
I earnestly believed.
You know this is an aside but
I'm tired of the previews for that latest *King Kong*
movie
Tired of all the actors looking to the sky with that
same
perplexed look,
That over the top awesome
because King Kong is computer generated

they can't see him
so they're really acting
and you know King is a thin veil for a Black man
America assuaging its racial fears.
Still, I'll pay ten, or twelve or twenty with popcorn
to see it.
There was a time too when I earnestly believed in
theatre
in performance
Believed I'd be a great big overnight success
that courage, innovation, tenacity would be recognized.
I earnestly believed
And I know there are those who will say I'm bitter
mislabel me
say I spew hatred
am raining down on their parade
That I lack optimism
when I try to say there is another America
when I try to say things are not equal
when I try telling them there are crimes
being carried out with doctors
many of them are modern criminals
who don't deserve white coats
There's another final solution that's occurring
right under our noses
and it's gonna get tougher and tougher
and tougher and tougher to hide the bodies

I earnestly believed
Saddam Hussein has been tried and convicted
but maybe it's just my secret silly wish
I keep wanting them to try George Bush
I keep wanting those feared 30,000 Iraqi soldiers dead
I want their bodies to rise up
walk to the White House
speak against this senseless war
For them to matter
to someone besides their mothers
I want those countless Americans killed little Black and
     Latino boys
I want all their lovers
Both women and men to tell what they've lost.
I want to see something like the truth and
reconciliation
hearings after apartheid
where this country must admit to committing atrocities
I want those millions of Americans living without health care
after working an entire lifetime...
I want seniors who can't afford their prescriptions
I want my parents to go
I want America's poor
ones who know about when hospitals and doctors
pull the plug on those who can't pay
I want the family of that little Black girl in New Orleans
whose body was found floating facedown

still wearing pink short shorts and a pink squeegee in
her hair.
Again, in New Orleans, I want the son whose mother
died during the floods
waiting for governmental help,
I want everyone to see the eyes of my student,
a black girl whose family is from the Ninth Ward in New
     Orleans
and how she looked the day in class when she said
they won't give us back our houses
want everyone to hear my friend when she said Bush
got up in the middle of the night to sign papers to help Terry
     Schiavo
but did nothing to help the people of New Orleans
I want every year for those gays and lesbians in New York
during Gay Pride
to stop dancing on the piers and form a political movement
I want all those voiceless people we're turning our
backs on
right now in the Darfur region of Africa to speak
And thank you Oprah, Thank you Bono, Thank you Jon Bon
     Jovi
for your generous donations
but the system has to change
Yes, there was a time when I earnestly believed
People get so defensive when I try telling them
what's happening systemically

when I say under this regime censorship has increased.
Artists no longer have spaces to work
nor money
and it's not just all about personal will
pulling oneself up by a bootstrap
There is marginalization and silencing
occurring across the board more than in other eras
perhaps this is a return to.
I honestly believed once that there were people more
enlightened
that competition and jealousy couldn't destroy our
world.
I believed helping a neighbor
was more important than money
I earnestly believed
Yes, by now I'm probably like someone in a horror film
who gets killed off easy
wasn't careful enough
Kept running toward instead of away
from the monster
The one who stayed in the haunted house
you know who goes into an attic or a basement
to investigate what's going on
when they should have been long gone, the one who
stays in an abusive cycle
believes the partner will change
The one who hasn't read all the signals

walks into a thieves den
like on the old 42nd St.
with money hanging out of their pockets.
I earnestly believed like Anne Frank in human good.
I believed the slogans I read in kindergarten
that policemen help you across the street
will return lost children to their parents.
Maybe I'm as naive as MLK
when he said he had a dream of what America could
become
Maybe he isn't here to witness
just how tough things have become
Integration is now only a small step or
small slice of what we need.
Yesterday I sat down in the sun
and let it beam across my face
I prayed like Martin Luther King
I could live one day in freedom
One day not racked by pain or injustice.
I felt like Harriet who lived in slavery
Just one day wanting to feel freedom's kiss
And caress.

Kong—Part 2

I have to go back in my mind
Because I saw that Kong movie last night

It was spectacular
except for the first hour which dragged on
and I almost walked out when the crew got to
Skull Island aka Africa
where Kong comes from
and I saw all those white oil painted actors playing natives
when everyone knows lots of Black actors need jobs
but the movie might have been even more offensive
if they'd cast them
Anyway, this Kong was an alpha if I've ever seen one—
He was like the Zulu warriors handling his business in
the jungle
Directed by the same guy who directed the Lord of the Rings
trilogy
this Kong gets medieval
There's a part where he snaps the neck and jaw of another
animal
then thrusts it aside
leaves the carcass
I mean this computer generated you could never guess was a
cartoon Kong
was so fierce
The American government could use him in their war to
fight Iraq
He could help them find looming terrorist at large
Osama Bin Laden
They could send him to change history

He could be like Rambo and try again to singlehandedly
win the Vietnam War—
Like Donald Trump, Charles Bronson, and Rambo rolled
into one
This Kong's got dominion
He's Shaft, a '70s icon
A private dick/ex-cop dispensing his own brand of
street justice
This Kong is like a Dominican warlord, not at all to be
    fucked with
I mean this Kong had that Fay Wray bitch climbing into
his hand
Excuse me, Naomi Watts
no argument, minimum screaming
What is it about sex or attraction to a good woman
that makes you want to beat your chest, go all
illiterate, yell oonga fucking boonga,
jump from the bushes, tie her up, dance with wolves,
unleash your inner self
Well this Kong is pure and unadulterated
He's some straight-up niggah, no rocks, no chaser
He's got a little of the fucked-up wild haired Ike
who told Tina
Don't you ever try to leave me
He's like Samuel Jackson on a bad day
Have you ever noticed how Sam Jackson, talented actor
that he is

plays the same character in every movie
He's perpetually angry
and excuse me for asking but what was he doing in the
Star Wars movie
He was like speaking Ebonics in space
You know how every syllable is over exaggerated and
drawn out
Like M-A-S-T-E-R S-O-L-O
I saw Sam's latest movie last night
Provocatively titled *Freedomland.*
All the acting screamed this is an important film
discussing race in America.
It's typical Hollywood fare
where complex human emotions
complex characters get reduced down to broad sketches
and caricature
not to mention everyone knows in 2007
parts of America are no better than Soweto during apartheid.
I mean come on I saw that new movie *Hustle and Flow*
sitting in the all-black audience
It was like back to days of segregated cinema/produced by
        MTV films
about a ne'er-do-well pimp/who just happens to also be
a rapper
trying to make it in America
The theme song just won an Academy Award called
It's hard out here for a pimp,

but everyone knows it's those who built America
slave labor.
I'll tell you this if you think I'm lying—
Stretching about this King Kong, Black man link
One of the white racist cops yells out to Samuel
Jackson's character
who is also a cop, You're supposed to be lord of the
jungle—
and then he points to a young black kid standing by
and says "So,
why aren't you handling this monkey?"
You've probably asked by now what's her investment
Why does she even care
and this is gonna get pretty painful
because I don't want to say
There were times right here in America
when I needed simple things like friendship, health care,
     love, resources
And I was made to live like an animal
Less than
Caged in
Speaking of pimps and hos
Can any of us ever forget the way Tina Turner was
treated by Ike
She was actually beaten with the heel of his shoe
Games, betrayals, sabotage, competition
Conscious and unconscious

Anything he could do to destroy her spirit
Not let her use that powerful beautiful voice she had
Except as a way for him to make money
I mean real moments where I've felt like this is
Cambodia 1975
And these are killing fields/like in the movie/the story of
that skinny war-torn reporter who gets left behind
while everyone else escapes
And all he tries to do every day is just survive
and I'm not the only one
with the way things are going
there will be more and more who'll one day
have to choose between their breakfast cereal
and taking their own lungs out
and if we don't watch out/this is the fall
the end of a once great civilization
a crumbling empire
I read recently in the paper
They found one of the Black men, a government official
dead in a ditch—
He was one of many who helped orchestrate the
Rwandan massacre
We all remember 1994 right
1/2 million dead
Black tribes in Africa warring against each other
And I can't believe I'm saying this about another
human being,

But I'm glad they killed that motherfucker
I'm glad he's dead
I have to go back again because I feel guilty that
earlier I mentioned Cambodia and killing fields
and the nature of that extermination
was so huge actually an estimated 1.7 million
but just today I read in the paper about a measure
being discussed in the Senate
on how to rid the United States of 12 million illegal
immigrants
and the language they used was rid.
The thing about this *King Kong* which differs from the
classic
is you can see what a great warrior he is
but a monster too
he's kind of human/contemplative
He actually manages in ape talk to sign the word
beauty
when they take him down/chloroform him
it's human beings/white people who look barbaric
when they put him on display
and you see his great paws
you know there isn't a theater big enough to contain
him
and the chains around his wrists represent all of our
greatness
both blacks and whites wrapped up in human bondage

all of our potential that's been lasso'd, corralled
Yeah, the only difference is when this Kong
Climbs on top of the Empire State Building to escape
Instead of seeing him shot down
Broken in captivity
This one, unlike the classic/that unruly inhumane
beast
This Kong—you want to be free

Kong—Part 3

It wasn't until I put posters up
handed out flyers of me, a 6 ft. 2 black woman
presiding over the city in a bra
while an image of King Kong lurked in the background
did I realize how long people had waited to see images of
    Kong usurped—
to see images we could laugh at/point fingers at/subvert.
It wasn't until then I realized how long King Kong had been
    lurking
in our cultural history/in our shadows/our shame.
Most of us know where he came from
from that birth of a nation era
born in 1933 from that great depression
where the Klu Klux Klan held dominance
not more than fifty years out of slavery

he was the story of slaves/a savage
brought here in chains/driven by his desire for a white
    woman.
He is the myth/the fear
just two years after the Scottsboro boys/twelve Black men
were accused of raping a white woman.
We continue to see him over and over in our movies
He is the subject of *To Kill a Mockingbird*
and the film just cause
he is the recent real-life story of a garbage man accused of
    raping
and murdering a white woman in a upper-middle-class
    neighborhood
as her five-year-old daughter stood by
he is the accused wilding wolf pack that went after
a Central Park jogger
And you wouldn't believe the responses I got
from people who weren't even followers of performance art
who weren't black clad
with purple hair or shaved heads
like the black security guard at LIU where I teach
who never gets involved in anything
saw the poster and said to me you go girl
Miss Foxy Brown, Cleopatra Jones
and then gives me a hug
and then the young black boy who works behind the counter
in the school cafeteria

who recognizes me from the poster
He says, Your piece looks interesting
and asks if I'm going to be playing King Kong or Fay Wray
and then the secretary in the school where I work
actually pulls notes she wrote out of her desk drawer she
        wrote
after seeing the Kong poster and says
I think he's a gentle giant.
And to her he is a symbol of good.
Then there are the more radical/expected/unexpected
        responses
like from the genteel black screenplay writer on my block
whom after I tell him casually I'm doing a piece on Kong
his face breaks into a disdain and grimace
as if he'd gone to the cinema and been betrayed
I brought my niece to see that new Kong film
I was so angry after I left/I wrote the producers a letter
which reminds me of another black man on my block/an
        investment banker
whom I've only ever seen planting flowers on the street
in boxes that aren't even his
he is genteel and middle class
and I thought to ask him what he thought
about what happened to blacks during the floods in New
        Orleans
and his face breaks into a Rubik's Cube I've never seen before
suddenly he thrusts his hands into the sky and starts to yell

It was wrong what they did to those people/it was wrong!
And all of this is coming from people
who would consider themselves to be ordinary people
not the lefties or revolutionaries
Even Donald Trump said the other day on television
President Bush has grossly mismanaged this country
and they found no weapons of mass destruction
and it all reminds me/shows me how under this regime
years of living under it has made a lot of us, everyday people
into heroes.
But the flower guy reminds me of something Audre Lorde
    said
in the book *Our Dead Behind Us*
She like the flower guy is gardening
but thinking of the violent deaths of black people in America
and then in her lover's country which is South Africa,
And she says,
My hand comes down like a brown vice over the marigolds
reckless through despair
we were two black women touching our flame
and we left our dead behind us.
Someone else sends me an article
about King Kong written by a man with my father's name
    James Snead
Someone else, a young white girl when she hears me recite
    King Kong
says excitedly and angrily

You should talk about how the FBI was an organization
built primarily to destroy radical movements.
Look what they did to the Panthers.
Someone else calls Peter Jackson a fascist
and I'm actually afraid to tell him I like the Lord of the Rings
    trilogy.
Someone else says you mentioned *Top Model*
will you talk about that
and I say I do in another piece
and then I try to prod people as gently as I can
and say these are your stories to tell now.
I simply pressed buttons, opened a door
but then something else comes to mind
that's unexpected after all is said and done.
Something that still haunts
I keep telling everyone who works on *Kong*
the video person and poster designer
make sure there's a skyline
we need images of the skyline it's important
since 9/11 I say the skyline/the city Kong stomped over
has changed
I'm aware now whether it's shown or not in pictures
something in our skyline is missing
Poet Sekou Sundiata said America lost her innocence
and it's true
it's like a jack-o'-lantern
someone took a knife and gauged out

a huge hunk of who we are
gone is our candyland
our jungle gym/our slide/our Tarzan-like swing
our playground of yesteryear
Poet Sekou Sundiata said America lost her innocence
and it's true.
And all I can say revisiting *Kong* trouncing through
all of the footage
suddenly the image of a great goliath
being taken down by tiny planes
has entirely new and different meaning.

credits and permissions

McLeod Chapman, and Daniel Gallant. From *The Best American Short Plays 2007–2008*.

Inquiries concerning rights should be addressed to cmcpumpkinpie@gmail.com.

Cruz, Migdalia. *Dreams of Home* (excerpts). Copyright © 1991 by Migdalia Cruz. From *Best American Short Plays 1991–1992*.

Inquiries concerning rights should be addressed to Ms. Peregrine Whittlesey at pwwagy@aol.com, or 279 Central Park West, New York, NY 10024.

Cunningham, Laura Shaine. *Web Cam Woman*. One of five monologues collected by Daniel Gallant under the heading *Five Story Walkup*, copyright © 2008 by John Guare, Neil LaBute, Quincy Long, Laura Shaine, Daniel Frederick Levin, Clay McLeod Chapman, and Daniel Gallant. From *The Best American Short Plays 2007–2008*.

Inquiries concerning rights should be addressed to laurashaine@gmail.com.

Fischer, Eileen. *The Perfect Medium* (excerpt). Copyright © 2008 by Eileen Fischer. From *The Best American Short Plays 2007–2008*.

Inquiries concerning rights should be addressed to daimon164@yahoo.com.

Frost, Polly, and Ray Sawhill. *The Last Artist in New York City*. Copyright © 2009 by Polly Frost and Ray Sawhill. From *The Best American Short Plays 2008–2009*.

Inquiries concerning rights should be addressed to pollyfrost. com, or raysawhill.com.

Levin, Daniel Frederick. *A Glorious Evening*. One of five monologues collected by Daniel Gallant under the heading *Five Story Walkup*, copyright © 2008 by John Guare, Neil LaBute, Quincy Long, Laura Shaine, Daniel Frederick Levin, Clay McLeod Chapman, and Daniel Gallant. From *The Best American Short Plays 2007–2008*.

Inquiries concerning rights should be addressed to danielflevin007@gmail.com or www.danielflevin.com.

Levy, Bruce. *Sada* (excerpt). Copyright © 2004 by Bruce Levy. From *The Best American Short Plays 2002–2003*. Inquiries concerning rights should be addressed to briane@mindspring.com.

Lovelace, Carey. *The Stormy Waters, the Long Way Home*. From *The Best American Short Plays 2008–2009*. Copyright © 2009 by Carey Lovelace.

Inquiries concerning rights should be addressed to Evan Ross Katz at evanrosskatz@gmail.com, or Loose Change Productions, 105 Duane Street, Suite 40D, New York, NY 10007.

Mack, Carol K. *The Courier* (excerpt). Copyright © 2005 by Carol K. Mack. From *The Best American Short Plays 2005–2006*.

Inquiries concerning rights should be addressed to www.carolmack.com.

Madden, Dano. *Beautiful American Soldier* (excerpts). Copyright © 2006 by Dano Madden. From *The Best American Short Plays 2005–2006*.

Inquiries concerning rights should be addressed to danomadden@gmail.com.

Maloney, Peter. *Leash*. Copyright © 2005 by Peter Maloney. From *The Best American Short Plays 2003–2004*. Witness. Copyright © 2005 and 2007 by Peter Maloney. From *The Best American Short Plays 2006–2007*.

Inquiries concerning rights should be addressed to Leading Artists, Inc., 145 West 45th Street, Suite 1000, New York, NY 10036.

Maruzzo, Joe. *Bricklayer's Poet* (excerpt). Copyright © 2008 by Joe Maruzzo. From *The Best American Short Plays 2007–2008*.

Inquiries concerning rights should be addressed to jpoetbrick@aol.com.

Medoff, Mark. *DeBoom: Who Gives This Woman?* (excerpts). Copyright © 2009 by Mark Medoff. From *The Best American Short Plays 2006–2007*.

Inquiries concerning rights should be addressed to markmedoff@comcast.net.

Miller, Susan. *Reading List* (excerpt). Copyright © 2005 by Susan Miller. From *The Best American Short Plays 2004–2005*.

Inquiries concerning rights should be addressed to www.susanmillerplaywright.com.

Mollenkamp, Julie Rae (Pratt). *In Conclusive Woman*. Copyright © 2006 by Julie Rae (Pratt) Mollenkamp. From *The Best American Short Plays 2006–2007*.

Inquiries concerning rights should be addressed to mollenkamp@ucmo.edu.

Other Monologue Books

Available from
Applause Books &
Limelight Editions

Childsplay
A Collection of Scenes and Monologues for Children
edited by Kerry Muir
Limelight Editions
9780879101886 .... $14.99

Duo!
The Best Scenes for Two for the 21st Century
edited by Joyce E. Henry, Rebecca Dunn Jaroff, and Bob Shuman
Foreword by Vivian Matalon
Applause Theatre & Cinema Books
9781557837028 .... $18.99

Duo!
Best Scenes for the 90's
edited by John Horvath, Lavonne Mueller and Jack Temchin
Applause Theatre & Cinema Books
9781557830302 .... $18.99

The Monologue Audition
A Practical Guide for Actors
by Karen Kohlhaas
Limelight Editions
9780879102913 .... $19.99

One on One
The Best Men's Monologues for the 21st Century
edited by Joyce E. Henry, Rebecca Dunn Jaroff, and Bob Shuman
Applause Theatre & Cinema Books
9781557837011 .... $16.99

One on One
The Best Women's Monologues for the 21st Century
edited by Joyce E. Henry, Rebecca Dunn Jaroff, and Bob Shuman
Applause Theatre & Cinema Books
9781557837004 .... $18.99

One on One: Playing with a Purpose
Monologues for Kids Ages 7-15
edited by Stephen Fife and Bob Shuman with contribuing editors Eloise Rollins-Fife and Marit Shuman
Applause Theatre & Cinema Books
9781557838414 .... $16.99

Scenes and Monologues from Steinberg/ATCA New Play Award Finalists, 2008–2012
edited by Bruce Burgun
The Applause Acting Series
Applause Theatre & Cinema Books
9781476868783 .... $19.99

Soliloquy!
The Shakespeare Monologues
edited by Michael Earley and Philippa Keil
Applause Theatre & Cinema Books
9780936839783 Men's Edition $11.95
9780936839790 Women's Edition $14.95

APPLAUSE
THEATRE & CINEMA BOOKS

AN IMPRINT OF

HAL•LEONARD®

Prices, contents, and availability subject to change without notice.